MW00448906

One
in Christ™

Applying Luther's Catechism

Student Guide

CONCORDIA PUBLISHING HOUSE · SAINT LOUIS

Copyright © 2003, 2012 Concordia Publishing House

3558 S. Jefferson Ave., St. Louis, MO 63118-3968

1-800-325-3040 • www.cph.org

All rights reserved. Unless specifically noted, no part of this publication may be reproduced, stored in a retrieval system, or transmitted, in any form or by any means, electronic, mechanical, photocopying, recording, or otherwise, without the prior written permission of Concordia Publishing House.

Editors: Scott and Julie Stiegemeyer and Rodney L. Rathmann; editorial assistant: Amanda G. Lansche

Scripture quotations are from the ESV Bible® (The Holy Bible, English Standard Version®), copyright © 2001 by Crossway Bibles, a publishing ministry of Good News Publishers. Used by permission. All rights reserved.

Excerpts from the catechism are from *Luther's Small Catechism with Explanation*, copyright © 1986, 1991 Concordia Publishing House.

Hymn texts with the abbreviation *LSB* are from *Lutheran Service Book*, copyright © 2006 Concordia Publishing House. All rights reserved.

The quotations from the Lutheran Confessions in this publication are from *Concordia: The Lutheran Confessions*, second edition; edited by Paul McCain, et al., copyright © 2006 Concordia Publishing House. All rights reserved. Brackets from *Concordia*.

This publication may be available in braille, in large print, or on cassette tape for the visually impaired. Please allow 8 to 12 weeks for delivery. Write to the Library for the Blind, 7550 Watson Rd., St. Louis, MO 63119-4409; call toll-free 1-888-215-2455; or visit the Web site: www.blindmission.org.

Manufactured in the United States of America

1   2   3   4   5   6   7   8   9   10   11   21   20   19   18   17   16   15   14   13   12

Contents

Unit 5—God's Grace for a New Life (Confirmation and the Table of Duties)

1 The Bible—God's Word to Us

A Look at the Bible

The Bible is the best-selling book of all time. Millions of copies have been printed and sold. All or parts of the Bible have been translated into more than a thousand languages. The Bible contains sixty-six separate books: thirty-nine in the Old Testament and twenty-seven in New Testament. It contains nearly twelve hundred chapters and almost thirty-one thousand verses.

1. Look at the first verse of the New Testament (Matthew 1:1). Who is mentioned there as the one who separated the Old and New Testaments?

2. What is the most important message of the Bible (John 3:16)?

3. The illustration on the right divides the books of the Bible according to the kind of writing they contain. Memorizing their names will help you find Bible references easily and quickly.
   Use the illustration to answer these questions:

a. Which five books of Moses tell of the life of God's people from creation through the wilderness wandering?

b. Which four New Testament books tell the story of Jesus' life?

c. Name the Old Testament hymnbook.

d. Which New Testament book tells what happened in the Christian Church after Jesus ascended into heaven?

4. How were the Bible books chosen? What criteria did the Early Church use to choose them?

1. Your best friend has let you down and told some secrets you shared.

2. You are facing a big test at school. You've studied a lot, but you are still nervous.

God's Word Has Power

Kevin finds out that the father of his friend Alex is an alcoholic. Kevin is concerned. He invites Alex and his family to church with him and his family. There, they hear the Gospel preached. Over time, the families become friends and Alex's family keeps coming to church.

Today, Alex's dad is participating in a support group, reading the Bible, going to Bible class, and taking adult instruction at church. If you ask Alex's dad why the change happened in his life, he'll say, "The Word of God did it."

3. Your mom or dad grounds you for something wrong that you did.

1. According to the following verse, what power does the Word (the Gospel) have? "For I am not ashamed of the gospel, for it is the power of God for salvation to everyone who believes, to the Jew first and also to the Greek" (Romans 1:16).

4. You are told by the doctor that you need surgery soon.

2. For what purpose has God's written Word been given? "I write these things to you who believe in the name of the Son of God that you may know that you have eternal life" (1 John 5:13).

Power in Your Life

You were changed, like Alex's dad, when you were baptized. And the changing goes on every day as the Spirit, through the Word, helps you repent, seek forgiveness, and live in service to God.

How might God help you through His Word in these situations?

To Review and Remember

Memorize the books of the Old and New Testament.

2 Law and Gospel— God Speaks to Us through His Word

A Very Great Message

Review Questions 1–8 the Introduction to the Catechism. Place the following words in the blanks below to make true sentences about the Christian faith and the Bible, God's Holy Word.

verbal inspiration	Greek
Jesus Christ	Aramaic
Hebrew	New Testament
Old Testament	error

Christianity is the life and salvation God has given us in and through _____ _____. God's truth about Jesus Christ is revealed in the _____ _____ , which promises the coming Savior, and the _____ _____ , which tells of the Savior who has come. We believe that God the Holy Spirit gave His chosen writers the thoughts that they expressed and the words they wrote. This belief is called _____ _____ . We believe the Bible is God's own Word and, as such, is without _____. The Old Testament was originally written in _____ and _____ . The New Testament was originally written in _____ .

Two Great Doctrines

God's Word can be divided into either *Law* or *Gospel*. We need to examine the words of the Bible to find these divisions.

God's *Law* tells us *what we should or should not do.*

The *Gospel,* however, tells *what God has done for us* because of His great love. The Gospel is the Good News of our salvation in Jesus Christ, through which God gives forgiveness, faith, life, and the power to serve Him in our lives.

Learn the italicized definitions of Law and Gospel to help you identify clear statements of them.

Read and think about each of the following statements from the Bible. Write *L* before each Law statement and *G* before each Gospel statement.

_____ 1. "He was wounded for our transgressions . . . and with His stripes we are healed" (Isaiah 53:5).

_____ 2. "And these words that I command you today shall be on your heart. You shall teach them diligently to your children" (Deuteronomy 6:6–7).

_____ 3. "You shall be holy, for I the LORD your God am holy" (Leviticus 19:2).

_____ 4. "What therefore God has joined together, let not man separate" (Matthew 19:6b).

_____ 5. "Christ loved the church and gave Himself up for her" (Ephesians 5:25b).

Use the same letters to identify Law or Gospel statements from life.

_____ 6. Jesus loves me, this I know.

_____ 7. Do unto others as you would have them do unto you.

_____ 8. We ought to obey God.

_____ 9. Heaven is a gift of God.

_____ 10. Jesus lived and died to save us from our sin.

God's Rules for Our Benefit

God knew we needed guidelines for our direction and protection, so He gave us rules to live by. He gave them to us because He loves us and knows what is best for us.

1. Look up the following Bible verses, and identify the two ways God has given us His Law.
a. Romans 2:14–15

b. Exodus 19–20; 31:18

2. Match each of the three types of law God gave with its description.

_____ Moral law

_____ Ceremonial law

_____ Political law

a. Regulated the religious practices in the Old Testament
b. Included the state law of the Israelites
c. Tells all people their duty toward God and other people

3. God established His moral law, the Ten Commandments, not only for Old Testament times, but also for our times. What happened, however, to the ceremonial and political laws (Galatians 2:16)?

God Is Love

Because God loves us, He sent Jesus to keep His Law perfectly in our place and to suffer, die, and rise again from the dead to pay the penalty our sins deserved. God's Spirit works in our lives to make us His forgiven people and to empower us to live according to His will. To assist us in our Christian life, our church has prepared a catechism. Review Questions 9–12 in *Luther's Small Catechism with Explanation* and fill in the following blanks.

A catechism is a book of instruction, usually in the form of _____ and _____. Our Small Catechism was written by _____ in _____. It sums up Christian doctrine by dividing it into the following Six Chief Parts:

All the chief parts of the Small Catechism are taken from the Bible, the only final authority for Christian faith and life.

To Review and Remember

The summary of Commandments 1–3 (First Table): Love the Lord your God with all your heart and with all your soul and with all your mind. *Matthew 22:37*

The summary of Commandments 4–10 (Second Table): And a second is like it: You shall love your neighbor as yourself. *Matthew 22:39*

For the law was given through Moses; grace and truth came through Jesus Christ. *John 1:17*

Through the law comes knowledge of sin. *Romans 3:20*

For I am not ashamed of the gospel, for it is the power of God for salvation to everyone who believes. *Romans 1:16*

3 The First Commandment—Putting God First

An Age-Old Problem

The First Commandment forbids the worship of false gods. People have worshiped false gods since the fall into sin. Some of them are listed in this acrostic:

Isis	Egyptian nature goddess
Dagon	Grain god of the Philistines
Odin	Norse god of war and wisdom
Loki	Norse god of mischief and trouble
Ashtoreth	Phoenician goddess of sexuality and fertility
Thoth	Egyptian god of wisdom and numbers
Ra	Egyptian sun-god and chief deity
Yoga	Hindu practice of self-discipline and meditation.

What word do we use to describe the worship of false gods?

(See the boldfaced letters.)

2. You might be surprised to discover that people still worship some gods of ancient times. The names have been changed, but many of the gods are the same.

a. Complete the following acrostic. Supply at least one other item beginning with the letter printed in bold that is something people today may love and honor more than the one true God.

Fame _____

Automobile _____

Land _____

Sex _____

Excellence _____

Gold _____

Outdoors _____

Discipline _____

Security _____

b. In what way(s) are some of these false gods the same as ancient idols?

3. Consider the following situations. What is wrong with the priorities of each person?

a. Amy grew up in a very poor home. When she got her first job at age fourteen, Amy was thrilled to be able to buy her own clothes. She then decided that the most important thing in life was to earn enough to buy all she wanted. She would save, go to school, and work extra hours at any kind of job so that she would never again have to go without something she wanted or needed.

b. Lin worked long hours and saved his money to buy a rusty sports car. Then, he spent every spare hour and every dollar he earned for materials to repair and restore it. After months of dedicated work, he drove his sparkling, shining treasure around the neighborhood for the first time. Even though it still took most of his time to keep it in perfect condition and nearly all of his money for gasoline and insurance, he loved the car so much he really didn't mind.

The First Commandment

You shall have no other gods.

What does this mean?

We should fear, love, and trust in God above all things.

Keeping the First Commandment

We keep the commandment when we follow the true God. How do we do this? Luther says we should *fear*, *love*, and *trust* in God above all things. Such is the desire God gives those who know and trust in Jesus as their Savior.

Tell how God would have us keep the First Commandment.

How do we FEAR God above all things?

1. Discuss: Which do you fear more—being rejected by your friends or being rejected by God? death or going to hell? Would you rather die for Christ or deny Him and be in danger of going to hell?

2. Read Luke 12:4–5. What does Jesus say about whom we should fear? Why?

3. Think about this illustration from Church history: When Polycarp was called before the Roman authority and told to worship him, he refused to do so, replying that he feared God and not the Roman ruler, in spite of the fire and wild animals the ruler held at his command to torture and kill him. Polycarp added that the torture and fire of the ruler would be but temporary but the fire awaiting all the wicked in the judgment to come will last forever. What motivated Polycarp?

How do we LOVE God above all things?

1. Discuss: What are some things that people love more than God? What about you? Do you love your family more than God? Do you love your life more than God? What would you be willing to die for? Would you, like Polycarp, be willing to die because of your faith—not from fear, but because you love Christ?

2. Read Mark 10:17–31. The young man came to Jesus looking for salvation. Why did he walk away

unhappy? What did he love more than God?

3. Read **Matthew 22:37**. What is the greatest commandment?

How do we TRUST in God above all things?

When we trust in God, we give up our control over our life and our own concerns about it. We give everything over to God. What do the verses in "Review and Remember" tell us about trusting in God?

To Review and Remember

Trust in the LORD with all your heart, and do not lean on your own understanding. *Proverbs 3:5*

For great is the LORD, and greatly to be praised; He is to be feared above all gods. *Psalm 96:4*

The First Commandment and its explanation

4 The Second Commandment— Honoring God's Name

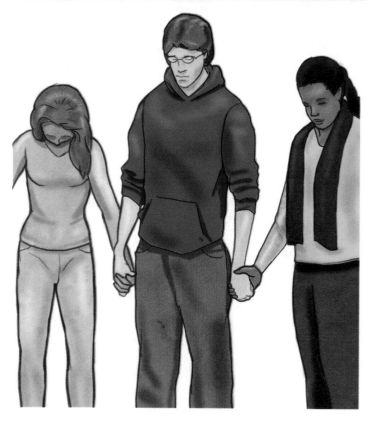

- **Swearing by His name.** This would be calling God as your witness to back up the truth of what you're saying. This is not how God wants us to use His name. He wants us to simply tell the truth.

- **Using satanic arts by His name.** This would be when we use Christian symbols or words or the name of God or Christ as good-luck charms. All forms of witchcraft and occultism are forbidden, even when it claims to be good.

- **Lying or deceiving by God's name.** This would be telling a lie about God or distorting God's Word. False doctrine is the teaching of unscriptural things about God.

Power in a Name

When you were baptized, God took you into His special family of faith and gave you His name. Because God is holy, He desires us to use His name for coming to Him in prayer, praise, and thanksgiving. He wants us to use His name to talk with others about His will for our lives and about His goodness to us. Sometimes, however, we misuse God's name in these ways:

- **Cursing with God's name.** This would be done by ordering God to send a person or thing to hell or by asking God to harm or hurt someone in His name.

The Second Commandment

You shall not misuse the name of the Lord your God.

What does this mean?

We should fear and love God so that we do not curse, swear, use satanic arts, lie, or deceive by His name, but call upon it in every trouble, pray, praise, and give thanks.

God Helps Us Honor Him with Our Use of His Name

Our loving God has given us all we are and have. Through the life, death, and resurrection of His Son, Jesus, He has made us His children by faith. He forgives our sins involving the misuse of His name and continues to shower His many blessings on us.

From what is printed on the next page, circle the words that show God's continued blessings to

His people. On a separate sheet, write a paragraph telling what these blessings mean for your life.

Psalm 103

Bless the Lord, O my soul, and all that is within me, bless His holy name!

Bless the Lord, O my soul, and forget not all His benefits, who forgives all your iniquity, who heals all your diseases, who redeems your life from the pit, who crowns you with steadfast love and mercy, who satisfies you with good so that your youth is renewed like the eagle's.

The Lord works righteousness and justice for all who are oppressed. He made known His ways to Moses, His acts to the people of Israel. The Lord is merciful and gracious, slow to anger and abounding in steadfast love.

He will not always chide, nor will He keep His anger forever. He does not deal with us according to our sins, nor repay us according to our iniquities.

For as high as the heavens are above the earth, so great is His steadfast love toward those who fear Him; as far as the east is from the west, so far does He remove our transgressions from us.

As a father shows compassion to his children, so the Lord shows compassion to those who fear Him. For He knows our frame; He remembers that we are dust.

As for man, his days are like grass; he flourishes like a flower of the field; for the wind passes over it, and it is gone, and its place knows it no more. But the steadfast love of the Lord is from everlasting to everlasting on those who fear Him, and His righteousness to children's children, to those who keep His covenant and remember to do His commandments.

The Lord has established His throne in the heavens, and His kingdom rules over all.

Bless the Lord, O you His angels, you mighty ones who do His word, obeying the voice of His word!

Bless the Lord, all His hosts, His ministers, who do His will!

Bless the Lord, all His works, in all places of His dominion.

Bless the Lord, O my soul!

Communicate!

What's the first thing you do when you have news to share? Whether it's good news or bad news, most of us first want to share that news with a friend. We call or text or tell a friend in person whatever our news may be.

Our loving God invites us to call on Him—at any time, for any reason. He is ready and able to help us with all our needs, large and small. Consider the following Bible references. Tell who called upon God in each situation. Then explain the reason for his or her call.

1. Psalm 18:1–3

2. Luke 1:28–31, 46–55

3. Luke 17:12–13

4. Luke 17:14–16

5. Acts 7:59–60

To Review and Remember

Call upon Me in the day of trouble; I will deliver you, and you shall glorify Me. *Psalm 50:15*

Selections from Psalm 103 printed in the lesson

The Second Commandment and its explanation

5 The Third Commandment— Worshiping God

A Family Reunion

Families need reunions. Today, our extended families are often spread out across the country, and when everyone in the family gets together, we have the opportunity to catch up and enjoy one another's company. Sometimes, extended families get together when there is a holiday, wedding, funeral, graduation, or confirmation. What happens at your family reunions? Do you eat together? share stories of the past? give gifts? What do you do together?

Somewhat similarly, when we come together as a family of God for worship on Sunday, we are coming to a family reunion. We are God's family. Our purpose in coming together is not just to have a good time, but also to strengthen family ties.

Many of the things we do at a family reunion sound much the same as those we do when we worship. Use the following as a guide to list what we do in worship.

1. What *meal* do we share in worship?

2. What *stories*, or *retellings of the past*, do we share in worship?

3. What things *do* we do together?

4. What *gifts* do we give and receive?

God's Family Reunions

When God created the world, He wanted people to rest as He did (Genesis 2:2–3), and He wanted people to worship Him at all times. But when God brought His people out of slavery in Egypt, He commanded them to worship Him specifically on that day of rest.

The ceremonial laws told them exactly what to do in worship and even how to construct their place of worship in order to help them look forward to the coming of the Messiah. The ceremonial laws no longer apply now that Jesus has come. So, today most Christians worship on Sunday as a reminder of the victory Jesus won for us when He rose from the dead on Easter Sunday.

Look at the following verses and tell which family reunion activity it refers to taking place during worship.

a. A meal
b. Stories or retellings of the past
c. Things we do together
d. Gifts we give and receive

1. Deuteronomy 5:15: You shall remember that you were a slave in the land of Egypt, and the LORD your God brought you out from there with a mighty hand and an outstretched arm. Therefore the LORD your God commanded you to keep the Sabbath day.

2. 1 Corinthians 11:23–25: For I received from the Lord what I also delivered to you, that the Lord Jesus on the night when He was betrayed took

bread, and when He had given thanks, He broke it, and said, "This is My body which is for you. Do this in remembrance of Me." In the same way also He took the cup, after supper, saying, "This cup is the new covenant in My blood. Do this, as often as you drink it, in remembrance of Me."

3. James 5:16: Therefore, confess your sins to one another and pray for one another, that you may be healed. The prayer of a righteous man has great power as it is working.

4. Psalm 147:1: Praise the Lord! For it is good to sing praises to our God; for it is pleasant, and a song of praise is fitting.

5. Colossians 3:16: Let the word of Christ dwell in you richly, teaching and admonishing one another in all wisdom, singing psalms and hymns and spiritual songs, with thankfulness in your hearts to God.

6. 2 Corinthians 9:7: Each one must give as he has decided in his heart, not reluctantly or under compulsion, for God loves a cheerful giver.

Discuss: Have you ever played the "trust game," where you fall backward into another person's arms? How did it make you feel to turn over control to someone else to save you? Is this similar to how we place our trust in God? Why or why not? Read Proverbs 3:5 and John 14:1 to help you answer these questions.

Read Isaiah 41:13 and Philippians 4:6. Why is it that we can trust the Lord? What does He promise? In these verses, we are told to do two things. What are they? How can we exercise our trust in Him when we have needs?

The Third Commandment

Remember the Sabbath day by keeping it holy.

What does this mean?

We should fear and love God so that we do not despise preaching and His Word, but hold it sacred and gladly hear and learn it.

The Third Commandment in the Christian Life

We worship God because He has given us life, the world in which we live, and everything we are and possess. His most important gift to us is the newness of life that is ours through our Savior, Jesus. When we worship God, two things happen: God gives blessings to us through the Word and Sacraments; we respond to His goodness in thankfulness. Identify each of the following as either God's gift (G) or our response (R).

_____ 1. A baby is baptized.

_____ 2. An offering is taken.

_____ 3. The people of God join together in corporate prayer.

_____ 4. The pastor reads God's Word to the congregation.

_____ 5. The congregation sings a hymn of praise.

_____ 6. The congregation receives Absolution for the sins they have just confessed.

_____ 7. The people receive Jesus' true body and blood in the Sacrament of the Altar.

_____ 8. The pastor explains and applies God's Word in a sermon.

_____ 9. The pastor pronounces the benediction.

_____ 10. The congregation says "Amen" to the prayers.

To Review and Remember

O Lord, I love the habitation of Your house and the place where Your glory dwells. *Psalm 26:8*

Let us consider . . . not neglecting to meet together, as is the habit of some, but encouraging one another, and all the more as you see the Day drawing near. *Hebrews 10:24–25*

The Third Commandment and its explanation

6 The Fourth Commandment— Respecting God's Representatives

Two Tables

We often divide the Ten Commandments into two parts, or tables. Jesus summarized the First Table in Matthew 22:37–38: "You shall love the Lord your God with all your heart and with all your soul and with all your mind. This is the great and first commandment." Jesus summarized the Second Table in Matthew 22:39: "And a second is like it: You shall love your neighbor as yourself."

1. Commandments 1–3 speak of love for _____.

2. Commandments 4–10 speak of love for _____.

3. The Fourth Commandment begins the Second Table of the Law, which is about serving our neighbor. So, who is our neighbor? Read the story of the Good Samaritan in Luke 10:29–37 to find out.

1. What does it mean to obey our parents in the Lord?

2. What does God tell parents to do?

God's Representatives Have Authority over Us

God rules and provides for the whole world. Sometimes, though, He rules and provides for His people through those He has placed in positions of authority over us. Parents are probably the authority closest to us. God loves, protects, and cares for us through them, as He has done since we were babies. God also tells us to honor and obey our parents.

> Children, obey your parents in the Lord, for this is right. "Honor your father and mother" (this is the first commandment with a promise), "that it may go well with you and that you may live long in the land." Fathers, do not provoke your children to anger, but bring them up in the discipline and instruction of the Lord (Ephesians 6:1–4).

3. According to the verses in Ephesians 6, what does the term "promise" mean?

4. God requires that we also honor all other authorities He has placed over us, including grandparents, aunts, uncles, babysitters, employers, pastors, and teachers. God also gives government leaders some of His power to rule people. Romans 13:1 tells us how God wants us to behave toward government, even though it may be as cruel and wicked as the Roman government was at the time of Paul: "Let every person be subject to the governing authorities. For there is no authority except from God, and those that exist have been instituted by God." So, why should we obey the government?

5. God wants us to give honor, respect, and support to presidents, governors, mayors, police, and other elected and appointed rulers, even though they sometimes make mistakes. We should also pray for them and use the freedom God has given us to influence government and to vote when we are of age. God tells us in His Word that there are particular situations in which we should not obey our parents or others in authority. According to Acts 5:29, what are these situations?

6. The Fourth Commandment does not give authority figures the permission to harm those who are in their care. For example, governments do not have the right to imprison the innocent or oppress the poor. Also, parents do not have the right to abuse their children or neglect them. The Fourth Commandment does not give the right to simply mistreat the people under their authority. Authority figures may have to discipline or punish but must avoid cruelty. What are some examples of times when authority figures might overstep their God-given role?

The Fourth Commandment

Honor your father and your mother.

What does this mean?

We should fear and love God so that we do not despise or anger our parents and other authorities, but honor them, serve and obey them, love and cherish them.

7. Think about the good things that our authorities give us. What blessings does God provide us through those placed in authority over us?

Examples of Honoring

The Fourth Commandment teaches that God is the ultimate authority. He puts parents, teachers, pastors, and others over us for our good. Further, He gives us faith and trust in Him. From that faith, we pour out our gratefulness to Him in a life of serving others. Consider the following situations. How could you show obedience to God in each one?

1. As you're walking out the door to go to a party next door, your parents tell you to be home an hour before it ends.
2. Your father warns you against unhealthy behaviors in which he himself indulges.
3. Your pastor cautions against a certain movie, but your best friend asks you to go see it.
4. You are outside when you notice a crabby neighbor struggling to lift a heavy box from her car.

To Review and Remember

Children, obey your parents in everything, for this pleases the Lord. *Colossians 3:20*

Hear, my son, your father's instruction, and forsake not your mother's teaching, for they are a graceful garland for your head and pendants for your neck. *Proverbs 1:8–9*

The Fourth Commandment and its explanation

7 The Fifth Commandment— Cherishing Human Life

The Fifth Commandment

You shalt not murder.

What does this mean?

We should fear and love God so that we do not hurt or harm our neighbor in his body, but help and support him in every physical need.

Killing vs. Murder

The Fifth Commandment forbids murder, but not all killing is murder. Murder, simply, is unlawful killing.

We never want to be in the situation where we have to kill, but not all killing is forbidden in this commandment. For instance, the Fifth Commandment does not forbid the killing of animals. God doesn't want us to be cruel, but it is not forbidden for us to kill animals for food or other uses. It is not breaking the Fifth Commandment to kill another human in self-defense, or while engaged as a soldier in war, or in capital punishment, when the government executes convicted criminals.

There are some clear guidelines from Scripture, however, that are examples of murder. Suicide is the taking of one's own life. Abortion and euthanasia are murder. Abortion is the voluntary removal and death of a preborn baby from the mother's womb. Euthanasia is the voluntary, unnatural death of someone (which could be doctor-assisted), usually for the very elderly or very ill.

1. Consider these two Bible stories in light of the Fifth Commandment.
a. Cain and Abel (Genesis 4:1–10). What happened?

Was the Fifth Commandment broken or upheld?

b. The Good Samaritan (Luke 10:29–37). What happened?

Was the Fifth Commandment broken or upheld?

2. Someone may tell you, "This is my body. I can do with it as I please—even end my life if I want to." God does not see it that way.
a. Read Deuteronomy 32:39 and 1 Corinthians 6:19. According to these statements from God, why is suicide forbidden?

b. How would you help a friend who talks about committing suicide?

c. What should you do if you have suicidal thoughts?

3. A teenage friend discovers she is pregnant. She is afraid to tell her parents. Someone suggests an abortion. You know that abortion is murder. You also want to help your friend. What do you say to her?

4. You are having a discussion about persons who are very elderly or otherwise unable to care for themselves. A classmate argues that painlessly ending those people's lives is the humane thing to do. How would you respond?

of Christ controls us, because we have concluded this: that one has died for all, therefore all have died; and He died for all, that those who live might no longer live for themselves but for Him who for their sake died and was raised" (2 Corinthians 5:14–15).

God desires that we not hurt or harm anyone in any way; it is His will that we treat one another with respect and care. Consider the following situations. Tell how, as the Holy Spirit works in your forgiven heart, you might show your love for God with regard to the Fifth Commandment, replacing feelings of greed, jealousy, guilt, and revenge with those of gratitude to God for His goodness to you in Christ Jesus.

1. Your kid brother has caused you trouble for years. He teases you constantly and embarrasses you in front of your friends. He's totally selfish. You've tried to be kind, but now your hurt is turning to hate. You can't stand him anymore. You don't want to be around him. Yet, you are a Christian. What is the answer? You might want to look at 1 John 4:19–21.

2. You've studied and worked hard. It wasn't easy, but you made the honor roll. Lisa, who has been jealous of you for a long time, told the teacher she saw you cheating on a test. The teacher doesn't change your grades, but her attitude toward you changes. She obviously believed the lie Lisa told, and you are hurt and angry. Your mom has been helping you plan a party for your friends. Lisa has always been a part of your crowd, and you are inviting all the others. What will you do about Lisa? You might want to look at Matthew 5:9–12.

The Life-Changing, Life-Saving Power of the Gospel

When God took upon Himself the body and life of a human, He showed that He held the quality of human life in high regard, that He was concerned enough to die for it. Now, by faith, God's children live their lives for Him. Writing by inspiration of the Holy Spirit, the apostle Paul explains, "For the love

To Review and Remember

Truly, I say to you, as you did it to one of the least of these My brothers, you did it to Me. *Matthew 25:40*

We love because He first loved us. If anyone says, "I love God," and hates his brother, he is a liar; for he who does not love his brother whom he has seen cannot love God whom he has not seen. And this commandment we have from Him: whoever loves God must also love his brother. *1 John 4:19–21*

The Fifth Commandment and its explanation

8 The Sixth Commandment—Practicing Godly Sex

The Sixth Commandment

You shall not commit adultery.

What dos this mean?

We should fear and love God so that we lead a sexually pure and decent life in what we say and do, and husband and wife love and honor each other.

God's Plan for You

God wants the best for you. He sent Jesus to win for you eternal life, which begins with your coming to faith and extends into eternity.

Until you join Him in heaven, He wants you to enjoy a full and complete life here on earth as the male or female He created you to be.

Sexuality is part of God's beautiful and perfect creation. When God looked at His creation of male and female, He pronounced it good. God had a plan for us right from the beginning. Read Catechism Question 55 and the following Bible verses. What is God's will for leading a sexually pure and decent life?

a. Genesis 1:27, 31

b. Genesis 2:24–25; Mark 10:6–9

c. Hebrews 13:4

d. Titus 2:11–12

The Plan Derailed

Sin marred God's plans for His people. Sin changed everything. The things that God created good turned bad. Happiness changed to sadness. Contentment changed to discontent. God's gift of sexuality became tarnished and exploited, misused and abused. The results of our misuse of God's gift of sexuality can easily be seen in the world around us. Studies show the following facts:

- By age 19, seven out of ten teens have had sexual intercourse.
- On average, young people have sexual intercourse for the first time by age 17 but don't get married until their mid-20s.
- Every second, over three thousand dollars is being spent on online porn.
- Sexually transmitted diseases run rampant in contemporary society.
- It is now socially acceptable to live together before marriage, and the number of couples co-habitating as opposed to getting married has risen drastically in recent years.
- Roughly 30–60 percent of all married people cheat on their spouses.
- More than half of all marriages end in divorce.

1. What hurtful consequences result from the preceding statements about our society?

2. From what specific offenses against the Sixth Commandment does God desire to protect us? Read Catechism Question 56 and the following Bible verses. Then, list sins against the Sixth Commandment as identified by the following Bible references.
   a. Ephesians 5:3–4

   b. Romans 1:24–28

   c. 1 Corinthians 6:18–20

A New Beginning

The Bible tells us that sinful thoughts originate in the heart and lead to sinful actions. Matthew 15:19 says, "For out of the heart come evil thoughts, murder, adultery, sexual immorality." Because of sin, we need a change of heart.

What changes your heart? See 1 John 1:7b.

What changes your life? See Psalm 51:10.

God's power in us can lead us from sinful actions to God-pleasing actions. What does the Bible tell us? See Ephesians 4:32–5:2.

A Chaste and Decent Life

There will continue to be pressure from friends and others, taunting you to give in and persuading you to do wrong. It's not easy to say no to temptation and stand up for what's right.

So, what's the alternative to following the "accepted practice" seen in movies, on television, and among both the respected and ordinary in the world around us? Seek the forgiveness, help, and power your loving God offers you through the Means of Grace. He promises to help. His Word says, "They who wait for the LORD shall renew their strength; they shall mount up with wings like eagles; they shall run and not be weary; they shall walk and not faint" (Isaiah 40:31).

As children of God, we need not follow the norm of our culture, but rather seek to honor God with our bodies. Some people practice abstinence out of fear of teen pregnancy or STDs, and these are real concerns to address. However, the Christian, out of love for God, trusts in Him to provide a spouse to love and cherish at the right time.

To Review and Remember

And whatever you do, in word or deed, do everything in the name of the Lord Jesus. *Colossians 3:17*

The Sixth Commandment and its explanation

9 The Seventh Commandment— Protecting Your Neighbor's Possessions

The Seventh Commandment

You shall not steal.

What does this mean?

We should fear and love God so that we do not take our neighbor's money or possessions, or get them in any dishonest way, but help him to improve and protect his possessions and income.

How God Sees It

"You shall not steal" is not as simple as it sounds. Identify the following as either something God requires (+) or forbids (-), according to the Seventh Commandment.

_____ 1. Actively help others take care of their interests and concerns (Philippians 2:4).

_____ 2. Be dishonest, specifically in regard to amounts (Leviticus 19:35).

_____ 3. Not repay or return what you've borrowed (Psalm 37:21).

_____ 4. Be generous and willing to share (1 Timothy 6:18).

_____ 5. Get something you haven't earned or don't deserve (2 Thessalonians 3:10).

_____ 6. Use tricks and lies to get something (Leviticus 6:2–3).

_____ 7. Help people who are in need (1 John 3:17–18).

_____ 8. Help or encourage someone else to do wrong (Proverbs 29:24).

a. 2 Corinthians 5:17

b. Psalm 5:8

c. Ephesians 2:10

How God Sees Us

When God looks at sin, what must He do? See Isaiah 13:11.

But when God looks at us—repentant believers— He doesn't see our sin. Instead, He sees Jesus, who was punished for us. Jesus is our gracious substitute (see 2 Corinthians 5:21). He forgives us and does so much more.

What happens in our lives through the power of Christ in us?

What Would You Do?

The forgiving and transforming power of Jesus in our hearts leads us to respect what belongs to other people and to help them protect and improve their possessions. Keep this in mind as you read the following comments. What would you do in the following situations?

I see someone drop a twenty-dollar bill and they don't notice. Do I give it back?

I borrow my friend's bike and break it. Then, I am embarrassed so I don't tell my friend. Is this stealing? Why or why not?

I have a huge essay due tomorrow but I haven't been able to start because of all of my other homework. I think I'll go online and buy an essay off the Internet. Is this okay? Is it breaking the seventh commandment?

On Halloween, someone leaves an entire bowl filled with candy on the porch with a sign that says: "Take one." How much do I take?

My friend loans me some earphones that I never give back. Is this stealing?

I'm so clever. I pretended that I hurt my back when I fell at the restaurant. Now they're giving me a big insurance settlement. Is this okay?

I get such a lousy salary. So I take things from work to even things out a bit. I just take little stuff they won't miss anyway. Is this breaking the seventh commandment?

I found a Web site where I can download music for free. I don't feel guilty because the rock stars are all rich anyway. Is this okay?

It's a Matter of Perspective

How we view other people's possessions is related to how we view what belongs to us. Possessions may appear to come to us through our work, as gifts from loved ones, as an inheritance, or by shrewd management. But Scripture says that "every good gift and every perfect gift is from above" (James 1:17).

God makes us managers of the possessions He entrusts to us. When God puts property into our care, He wants us to do more than just keep it for our own use. Property is an investment that God wants us to use to benefit others: "Do not neglect to do good and to share what you have, for such sacrifices are pleasing to God" (Hebrews 13:16).

The Holy Spirit helps us to be good stewards of all He has given us. He enables and empowers us as He works in us through the Means of Grace—God's Word and the Sacraments. Because we love the giver of all good gifts, and because we serve Him by serving others, we can show our love for God by helping people care for what belongs to them and by sharing what we have with others. List ways you can help people in your home, school, church, and community.

To Review and Remember

Let each of you look not only to his own interests, but also to the interests of others. *Philippians 2:4*

The Seventh Commandment and its explanation

10 The Eighth Commandment— Protecting Your Neighbor's Reputation

Think of your good qualities, talents, and personality. Describe what you would like your reputation to be. In other words, if you moved to another town, how would people remember you? Describe this in two or three sentences.

Think about your attitude toward the people in your life—your parents, siblings, and friends. How do you speak about them, and how do you affect their reputations?

Looking at Yourself

What is a reputation? You can't see, feel, hear, taste, or smell it, but everyone has one. And most people care a lot about it: "A good name is to be chosen rather than great riches, and favor is better than silver or gold" (Proverbs 22:1).

Your reputation is the story of who you are. A good reputation can make you trustworthy and accepted. A bad reputation can make others suspicious and distrustful of you. Consider your reputation. How do people view you? For example, let's say you were trying to get babysitting jobs. Would your reputation help you or hurt you?

Consider the following:

Babysitter A has been known to be a poor student, and the rumor is that he stole money from his last babysitting job.

Babysitter B is active in Girl Scouts, youth group, and recently played an instrument at church on Christmas Eve.

A reputation is a tricky thing. Babysitter A could be innocent of the stealing and just had a rough semester, while Babysitter B could be doing all of the right things outwardly but loves to gossip and laugh about her friends behind their backs. The bottom line is that a reputation is all about how people perceive you—what they think about you as a person.

The Eighth Commandment

You shall not give false testimony against your neighbor.

What does this mean?

We should fear and love God so that we do not tell lies about our neighbor, betray him, slander him, or hurt his reputation, but defend him, speak well of him, and expla[i]n everything in the kindest way.

A Serious Concern

God knows how important and also how fragile a reputation can be, so He gives us this commandment.

The Book of Proverbs further explains this commandment. Draw lines between phrases in the following box to match up actions, adjectives, and proverbs that go together.

A Person Who Tells	Is	See
what is unreliable	unkind	Proverbs 11:[1]
what is personal	untrustworthy	Proverbs 17:[9]
what is negative	unfaithful	Proverbs 18:[2]

How God Sees Us

What is your reputation with God? Look at the Eighth Commandment as a mental checklist. Think about times you have said things that hurt other people. How do you look from the viewpoint of the Law? See James 3:2.

1. **Poison:** "Did you see what John wrote about Ashley on Facebook last night? It's all over the Internet now that she shoplifted from the grocery store and got caught."
Antidote:

Not one of us is perfect. According to the Law, we are not loving or lovable. Unworthy though we are, God still loves us. He redeemed us and made us worthy to be called His children once again, through Jesus' life, death, and resurrection. How do you look from the viewpoint of the Gospel? See 2 Corinthians 5:17.

2. **Poison:** "I can't wait to tell you what I saw. Jason flunked the test and got Saturday detention. He was so embarrassed."
Antidote:

The love of God leads us to lovingly speak well of others. Love defends when others accuse. Love speaks kindly when others find fault. Love speaks positively when others speak negatively. Love looks for kind explanation in the face of suggested wrong. And love is silent when there is no clear good thing to say.

3. **Poison:** "Did you hear that Kelly's father was called on by Children and Family Services? The rumor is that he beats his kids. Kelly says he's innocent. But why would they accuse him if he didn't do it?"
Antidote:

What's the Remedy?

Read James 3. Verse 8 tells us that words can be like a deadly poison. In God's Word, we also find the antidote to that poison. Reread verse 17 and complete the following sentence:

Through the power of the Holy Spirit working in us, we can speak words that are

4. **Poison:** "You broke it! Well, just blame it on Jason. No one ever trusts him anyway."
Antidote:

5. **Poison:** "Marcy made the cheerleading squad. It sure can't be because she's good. It's probably because her dad paid off the coach."
Antidote:

In each of the following situations, write a response that considers God's will for our words and shows compassion.

To Review and Remember

[Love] does not rejoice at wrongdoing, but rejoices with the truth. *1 Corinthians 13:6*

Let your speech always be gracious . . . so that you may know how you ought to answer each person. *Colossians 4:6*

The Eighth Commandment and its explanation

11 The Ninth and Tenth Commandments—Being Content

The Ninth Commandment

You shall not covet your neighbor's house.

What does this mean?

We should fear and love God so that we do not scheme to get our neighbor's inheritance or house, or get it in a way which only appears right, but help and be of service to him in keeping it.

The Tenth Commandment

You shall not covet your neighbor's wife, or his manservant or maidservant, his ox or donkey, or anything that belongs to your neighbor.

What does this mean?

We should fear and love God so that we do not entice or force away our neighbor's wife, workers, or animals, or turn them against him, but urge them to stay and do their duty.

A Heart Condition

Wanting something isn't necessarily wrong. What does Jesus tell us in Matthew 7:7 about the things we want?

However, wanting becomes a problem when we long for something that God has not given us. For example, we want our parents to drive a better car so we look cooler when we're dropped off for volleyball practice. We want a bigger house so that our place will be the hangout spot. We want the custom-made basketball shoes with the colors and design of our choosing. We want. We want. We want!

Coveting means that we want something God has not already provided for us. He has given us a car, a home, and shoes, but we always want something better, something cooler, something more.

Coveting makes us greedy for more and discontent with what we have. When we covet, our will moves God's will out of our lives. Instead, God tells us to be at peace, to be content with what He has given.

God's Word tells us we should not only avoid coveting, but we should also learn to be content with what we do have.

1. Read 1 Timothy 6:8–10. In these verses, what is the writer content with having? What is the problem with people who want to get rich?

2. Read Luke 12:15. Unlike our culture, which tells us to get more and more "stuff," what does the Gospel writer say that our lives are *not* made of?

3. Read Hebrews 13:5. According to this verse, why should we be content with what we have?

Avoiding coveting does not necessarily mean that we should not work toward a better life. Many people barely make enough money to feed their families and put a roof over their heads. Instead, God wants us to be wise with money, to take care of our households, and to give generously. He wants us to be content with all of the many blessings He has given.

But sometimes our ordinary interests turn into sin when we yearn for the things that are not ours. Discuss the following scenarios, and respond to the questions that follow.

a. *Natalie and Jacklin were best friends. They were also friends with Keiko, but they did not always include her. What could Keiko be feeling during these times that could lead to coveting?*

b. *You saw all your friends on Facebook posting their Christmas presents. A bunch of kids got the latest electronic gadget. What would your re-*

sponse be if you coveted their good fortune?

c. More than anything, Josh wanted to make it onto the baseball team. He worked hard practicing his swing and working on his pitching. If he didn't make the team, what covetous attitudes or behaviors might he show?

Think about these scenarios. Is there a fine line between admiring someone else's success and coveting it?

Too often, we do not recognize or want to admit when we have crossed over the line from wanting something to coveting (wanting what belongs to someone else and even plotting to get it). So God has given us the Law to show us His will. Paul writes in Romans 7:7, "Yet if it had not been for the law, I would not have known sin. For I would not have known what it is to covet if the law had not said, 'You shall not covet.'"

We need help, and help we have through the cross of Christ. God is ever faithful, even though by sinning we have been unfaithful. What does God's Word promise to us? See 1 John 1:9.

God calls us to repentance—to confess and turn from our sin and live as His people. We are enabled to do this through the power of the Holy Spirit working in us.

Ever Faithful

God is our example of faithfulness, and He desires that we be His faithful people. Led by the Holy Spirit, we will be faithful in our relationships with others and encourage them to remain faithful in their own relationships.

In the story situations discussed earlier, how could the people have responded in a way that encouraged faithfulness, loyalty, honesty, and responsibility?

a.

b.

c.

In all of these cases, the people involved can speak the Good News of Jesus and His love. Rather than seeing jealousy and unfaithfulness destroying relationships, God desires to see people come to faith and live in unity and peace in Christ. Read aloud together Romans 15:5–6.

A Change of Heart

It's hard to be content because often what we want and what God wants are two different things! What does that tell us?

Only Jesus can turn us from following our own will to following God's will. He calls us to repentance. He offers forgiveness through His death on the cross. He offers a clean heart through the power of the Holy Spirit.

The Bible tells us that as God looked for a new king for Israel, the Lord "sought out a man after His own heart" (1 Samuel 13:14). God's choice was David—a sinner, but one in whom God had created a clean heart and renewed a right spirit (see Psalm 51:10). Because the Lord redeems and sanctifies you, you, too, can be a person "after His own heart." What is it like to be that kind of person?

To Review and Remember

Keep your life free from love of money, and be content with what you have, for He has said, "I will never leave you nor forsake you." *Hebrews 13:5*

The Ninth Commandment and its explanation

The Tenth Commandment and its explanation

12 The Close of the Commandments—A Summary

Reviewing the Commandments

Read and review the statements below. Decide if the person in each statement is keeping or breaking the commandment and which commandment it is. So, answer two questions about each example: (1) Does this example show someone keeping or breaking a commandment? (2) Which commandment does it keep or break? Fill in the chart to show your answers.

a. "I don't understand what the big deal is," Sydney said. "Aren't Jesus and Muhammad kind of the same?"

b. Even though he was tired, Connor got up and went to church and Bible class.

c. Ian downloaded a song for free from a pirated Web site.

d. "I don't care what my mom says," Kelly promised. "I will go to that party even if I have to sneak out of the house."

e. Haley sent a picture message of herself in a barely-there bikini to her boyfriend.

f. When a pop-up ad for porn opened up on John's computer screen, he closed it right away.

g. "Did you hear that Rebecca made it onto the lacrosse team? I'm really happy for her."

h. "Look at that Lamborghini," Mike said. "Why can't we get a car like that, Dad? I hate my life."

i. "I hate him so much!" Jen cried. "I wish he were dead."

j. Laura called on God's name when she was afraid.

Commandment	Example keeping commandment	Example breaking commandment
1		
2		
3		
4		
5		
6		
7		
8		
9–10		

We Stand Accused

God is just. He cannot condone, or allow, sin because He is holy. God's holiness makes it impossible for Him to turn the other way and ignore our sin. In order to satisfy justice, punishment must be sentenced.

Think of it like a courtroom. Let's say a child murderer is convicted of his crime. It is proven beyond the shadow of a doubt that this individual committed this terrible act. What if, after the conviction, the judge or jury said, "Oh well, boys will be boys. Just try not to do it again." How do you think the parents of the murdered child would feel?

God's standard of justice is even more stringent. Our human judgment may fail because we are prone to bias and error. But God's ways and judgments are perfect.

God's Law shows us that we are guilty. It confronts us with our sins. And God hates sin. What are the consequences of sin? See Catechism Question 70.

The Old Testament tells again and again how God acted because of impenitent sinfulness. Sometimes, His acts of punishment were swift and terrible, as when the children of Israel worshiped the golden calf. At other times, the punishment came after many years and many warnings, as when Jerusalem fell and Judah was carried away to Babylon. Some impenitent sinners are not punished until they spend eternity in hell. But in His own way and at His own time, *God punishes impenitent sinners.* God's anger at sin is righteous and powerful. Read about it in Job 9:10–15. Ultimately, what does Job say is the only thing we sinners can do?

CAUSE	EFFECT
People spoke against God.	Numbers 21:6
People grieved the Lord.	Genesis 6:17
God's love is unending.	1 Peter 3:18

The Close of the Commandments

What does God say about all these commandments?

He says: "I, the Lord your God, am a jealous God, punishing the children for the sin of the fathers to the third and fourth generation of those who hate Me, but showing love to a thousand generations of those who love Me and keep My commandments." (Exodus 20:5–6)

What does this mean?

God threatens to punish all who break these commandments. Therefore, we should fear His wrath and not do anything against them. But He promises grace and every blessing to all who keep these commandments. Therefore, we should also love and trust in Him and gladly do what He commands.

God Is Just

Justice demands consequences. Thank God He is more than just! Thank God He is also merciful! Sin must be punished by death—that is justice. So God sent His Son, Jesus, to take the punishment for our sins by dying on the cross so that we may live with Him in heaven—that is mercy. Read Romans 6:23, which speaks of this same cause-and-effect relationship. In your Bible, circle each cause and draw an arrow to each effect.

To Review and Remember

May the God of endurance and encouragement grant you to live in such harmony with one another, in accord with Christ Jesus.That together you may with one voice glorify the God and Father of our Lord Jesus Christ. *Romans 15: 5–6*

The close of the Commandments and its explanation

13 The Purpose of the Law— To Bring Us Back to God

Civil Law

Civil laws are laws that the government makes. The civil laws in Leviticus 19–20 and 24–27 were given specifically to the people of Israel who, after the exodus, were no longer under Egyptian law. Israel's form of government was a theocracy—direct rule by God. The civil laws were very strict; God made them to protect His people from falling into the evil ways of their wicked neighbors.

Many years later, the people chose to have a monarchy—government ruled by a king. God in His love then ruled through His representatives, who made their own laws.

1. What is God's will for us regarding civil authorities? See Romans 13:1–7.

2. What qualification is given in Acts 5:29?

Ceremonial Law

The ceremonial laws concerned the worship life of God's people.

WHO? Who led the worship celebration? See Numbers 3:10, 32.

WHAT? What were some of the parts of worship? See 2 Chronicles 29:31 and Psalm 69:13, 34.

WHERE? Where did ceremonial worship take place? See Psalm 27:4–6.

WHEN? When did this worship take place? See Leviticus 23:3–10, 23–24, 26–27, 33–44.

WHY? The Old Testament ceremonies of purification, sacrifices, and feast days reminded the people of their sins and their need for a Savior. The celebrations offered God's forgiveness and pointed to and prefigured the saving work of the promised Messiah—Jesus Christ.

WHY NOT? Why don't we continue to use the Old Testament ceremonial laws? See Hebrews 10:1–7, 10, 14, 18.

Moral Law

The civil and ceremonial laws were for certain people at a certain time. We no longer follow those laws. But God does want us to obey the moral law—the Ten Commandments. Jesus spoke about the moral law in the Sermon on the Mount. Read Matthew 5:17–19 and fill in the missing words of this paragraph:

Jesus came into the world to _____ the Law, not to _____ it. Until the end of the world, no part of the Law shall be changed or removed until all things are _____. God does not want us to _____ [break] any of the commandments. Instead, He desires that we do _____ and _____ them.

Imperfect though we may be, we often have a purpose for the things we do. God, who is perfect, always has a purpose for the things He does. Let's take a closer look at God's purposes for giving the moral law.

God's Law as a Curb

According to Catechism Question 77, part A, how does the Law serve as a curb?

A curb stops you from going the wrong way; it keeps you from going the wrong direction. The Law does the same. **It tells us what we should not do.** To whom does God's Law give this message? See 1 Timothy 1:9.

Who is included? See Ecclesiastes 7:20.

God's Law as a Mirror

According to Catechism Question 77, part B, how does the Law serve as a mirror?

It tells us that we have done what we should not do.

Consider the case of someone who looks in the mirror of the Law and says, "It looks like I'm doing pretty well! I'm a nice person, and I always try to do the right thing." What does God's Word say about that? See 1 John 1:8 and Isaiah 64:6.

The Law as a mirror not only shows us our sin but also shows our hopeless condition. **It tells us that we need someone to save us.**

God's Law as a Guide

While the Law shows us our sin and our need for help, the Gospel gives us the Good News of Jesus, our Savior. Jesus obeyed the Law, took the penalty of the Law, and fulfilled the Law for us! By doing this, He has put an end to the Law (Romans 10:4). Jesus has freed us from the Law as a curb and as a mirror. So now, as redeemed people of God, we can look at the Law in a new way—as a guide. According to Catechism Question 77, part C, how does the Law serve as a guide?

To Review and Remember

Your word is a lamp to my feet and a light to my path. *Psalm 119:105*

Give me understanding that I may learn Your commandments. *Psalm 119:73*

Let Your steadfast love come to me, O LORD, Your salvation according to Your promise. *Psalm 119:41*

14 Sin—Our Problem; Forgiveness—God's Solution

Defining Sin

What is sin? Theologians throughout the centuries have worked to define sin and break it into different categories to help us understand it. Read the following descriptions and answer the questions.

1. **Original Sin.** Read Psalm 51:5 and Genesis 8:21. Think about a tiny baby. Is he or she sinful? Explain your answer.

Sin is part of our natural condition. This is not an excuse; it is a reality. It has been passed from all parents to all children since our first parents, Adam and Eve, fell into sin: "Sin came into the world through one man" (Romans 5:12). If we are born in sin, our one hope is to be born again.

2. **Actual Sin.** If original sin is the "disease" or condition we are born with, then actual sins are the "symptoms" or demonstrations of the disease. If we have original sin "by nature," then we have actual sin "by will." There are three types of actual sins—in thoughts, in words, and in deeds. What are some examples of actual sins?

3. **Commission and Omission.** Actual sins may be sins of commission (doing what is wrong) or sins of omission (not doing what is right). Sins of commission are often easy to identify. Sins of omission may go undetected, even by the person in error. Write three scenarios or sample situations that show sins of omission.

a. In thinking (an example: Lucy couldn't stop thinking about her own problems and didn't even notice that her friend was trying to get her attention when she needed help):

b. In speaking (an example: Instead of apologizing for her angry comments, Alyssa was quiet and avoided her friend):

c. In action (an example: Steven knew his neighbor needed help carrying her groceries in her house, but he pretended not to see her and instead went into his own house):

Forgiveness, Life, and Salvation

The penalty for sin is death. Jesus paid that penalty for us when He died on the cross. Jesus not only died for us, but He also lived for us. He lived for us *before* and *after* He died on the cross. In the yellow box at the top of the next page, write the purpose for Jesus' life before and after His death on the cross.

Jesus lived for us, and He desires that we live for Him. Read Galatians 2:20; James 4:7; Romans 6:1–2; Galatians 5:13; 2 Corinthians 5:17. Knowing this, how can you respond to these excuses for sin?

Before Jesus died on the cross, He lived in order to

After Jesus died on the cross, He lived in order to

Romans 5:19;
John 13:15

Romans
6:4–11

a. "The devil made me do it."

1.

b. "It doesn't matter. God will always forgive me."

2.

c. "I can't help it. I am sinful by nature."

3.

Do you see how the words connected by arrows relate to each other? Use each new pair of words in a sentence that shows this relationship.

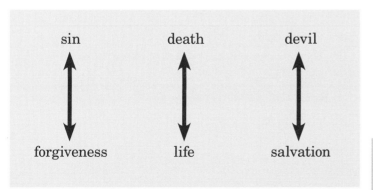

THROUGH CHRIST, THE VICTORY IS OURS! LIVE FOR THE LORD!

To Review and Remember

Be strong in the Lord and in the strength of His might. *Ephesians 6:10*

Thanks be to God, who gives us the victory through our Lord Jesus Christ. *1 Corinthians 15:57*

15 The Apostles' Creed—I Believe

Creeds of the Church

The word *creed* comes from the Latin word *credo,* meaning "I believe." The Apostles' Creed is so named because it dates back almost to the time of the apostles, perhaps as early as AD 120, when it was used as a summary of the central doctrines to be taught and preached in the Church. It also was used as a personal confession of faith for people who were about to be baptized as adults. The Apostles' Creed is the earliest of the three general creeds of the Church. The second general creed is the Nicene Creed, and the third is the Athanasian Creed.

List ways you think creeds might be useful to God's people today.

God: Father, Son, and Holy Spirit

The main confession of all three of our Christian Creeds is the belief in the Holy Trinity: Father, Son, and Holy Spirit—three distinct persons in one divine being. Even though the word *Trinity* is not actually in the Bible, the teaching of God in three persons definitely is.

There are three persons of the Trinity—Father, Son, and Holy Spirit—but only one God. This teaching of the Holy Trinity is difficult for us to grasp in

our limited understanding. But this is the mystery God has revealed to us.

Let's look at some Bible verses that describe each person of the Trinity. Read the following verses and tell which persons of the Trinity are described.

There are three persons . . .

1. Matthew 28:19

2. John 15:26

. . . but one God
Deuteronomy 6:4 and 1 Corinthians 8:4 (summarize these verses).

One common error people believe about the Trinity is that it is one person with three "masks" or "jobs." Think of an actor in a theater who wears three different masks. It's the same person, but he's playing three different roles. This is not a correct Christian teaching. Instead, the Holy Trinity shares a unity of being—one God in three persons simultaneously.

In this lesson, we focus on the First Person of the Trinity, God the Father. Without exception, our earthly fathers are imperfect people. Our heavenly Father is the perfect parent, loving each of us unconditionally and always wanting the best for us. His gift of Jesus to be our Savior evidences the extent of His great love.

Read the following verses and summarize:

1. John 20:17

2. Galatians 3:26

3.   Ephesians 3:14–15

I Believe

An important part of Christian living is to be able to say and mean, "I believe." Of greatest importance, however, is *what* a person believes. This truth is not widely accepted. There are many people who believe that it really doesn't matter what you believe as long as you believe it sincerely. Read what God says in Acts 4:12. Then write in your own words what you have learned about the importance of believing only the truth.

Two confessions from the Bible also illustrate this point. Read each Bible account and answer the questions below.

Luke 9:18–20

Who is speaking?

What is being confessed?

John 11:17–27

Who is speaking?

What is being confessed?

Words Are Not Enough

Words of confession are very important, but they are not as important as the faith that lies behind the words. Matthew 7:21 warns, "Not everyone who says to Me, 'Lord, Lord,' will enter the kingdom of heaven, but the one who does the will of My Father who is in heaven." Spoken by a child of God, "I believe" means more than that the speaker accepts the truth of what he or she says. The "believing" of saving

faith can be illustrated by a triangle. If any one side is missing, the triangle ceases to exist. So it is with faith. Summarize the message of each Bible reference within the triangle in a single word. Write that word on the correct side of the triangle.

The Apostles' Creed

I believe in God, the Father Almighty, Maker of heaven and earth.

And in Jesus Christ, His only Son, our Lord, who was conceived by the Holy Spirit, born of the Virgin Mary, suffered under Pontius Pilate, was crucified, died and was buried. He descended into hell. The third day He rose again from the dead. He ascended into heaven and sits at the right hand of God, the Father Almighty. From thence He will come to judge the living and the dead.

I believe in the Holy Spirit, the Holy Christian Church, the communion of saints, the forgiveness of sins, the resurrection of the body, and the life everlasting. Amen.

James 2:19   Psalm 37:5

FAITH

Romans 10:14, 17

To Review and Remember

Now faith is the assurance of things hoped for, the conviction of things not seen. *Hebrews 11:1*

So faith comes from hearing, and hearing through the word of Christ. *Romans 10:17*

The Apostles' Creed

16 The First Article—Creation

In the Beginning Was . . .

Since the earliest times, people have asked, "How did the world get here?" Sometimes people used their minds and their imaginations to answer this question. Such human explanations are called *myths* (if they are made-up stories) or *theories* (if they are based on reason). We may laugh at some of the ancient stories and be challenged by the theories of the present, but the question remains, "How did the world get here?"

Since we were not present at the beginning, the best way to get a correct description of that time is to hear the report of someone who was present, someone perfectly reliable.

1. Read the verses below and tell who was present at the world's beginning:
a. Psalm 90:2

b. John 1:1

c. Genesis 1:2

2. Why do many not believe in God as the Creator and Ruler of the world? See Hebrews 11:3.

- The universe began without an outside agent in an explosion, the Big Bang.
- Life as we know it came into being by chance, from a "primordial soup," or a mix of chemicals.
- Species, such as humans, came from one ancestor and evolved from successive random mutations over millions of years.

These ideas are in basic conflict with the teachings of the Bible:

- God created the universe. It was not random, but planned.
- God created all life.
- Human beings were created specially by God, in His likeness and image.

So, how do we deal with these differences in our science classes, in our discussions with other people, and in our own thoughts and feelings?

First, we *listen*. Make sure that when you come across people with a different worldview, you listen to their side of the argument. They probably believe their theory as strongly as you believe yours.

Second, we *discern*. Discerning means to listen

What's Wrong with Evolution?

Many people today have bought into the theory of evolution. This theory is taught in our schools, defended by scientists, and assumed to be true by most people in the scientific world. But how do we as Christians, who believe in the reliability and truth of the Bible, which teaches a six-day creation, approach this theory and share our own beliefs with others?

First, we must understand the basic teachings of evolution.

with understanding. As students, we do not simply accept everything we are taught. We examine our thoughts and beliefs, and we compare what others say to what we know to be the truth.

Third, we *continue to learn*. As confirmation students, you are thinking and learning about many teachings and doctrines for the first time. But as Christians, you are lifelong learners. You never cease to learn about God's Word and how God works in the world.

I Believe in God, the Father Almighty, Maker of Heaven and Earth

Let's break apart the pieces of this First Article. Read each section and the Bible verses given. Summarize what they say.

1. "I believe"; John 6:28–29; Habakkuk 2:4

2. "in God"; Isaiah 6:3; Exodus 34:6–7

3. "the Father Almighty"; Malachi 2:10; John 3:18

4. "Maker of heaven and earth"; Psalm 33:6, 9; Hebrews 11:3

The First Article—Creation

I believe in God, the Father Almighty, Maker of heaven and earth.

What does this mean?

I believe that God has made me and all creatures; that He has given me my body and soul, eyes, ears, and all my members, my reason and all my senses, and still takes care of them.

He also gives me clothing and shoes, food and drink, house and home, wife and children, land, animals, and all I have. He richly and daily provides me with all that I need to support this body and life. He defends me against all danger and guards and protects me from all evil. All this He does only out of fatherly, divine goodness and mercy, without any merit or worthiness in me. For all this it is my duty to thank and praise, serve and obey Him.

This is most certainly true.

To Review and Remember

In the beginning, God created the heavens and the earth. *Genesis 1:1*

The Lord God formed the man of dust from the ground and breathed into his nostrils the breath of life, and the man became a living creature. *Genesis 2:7*

By faith we understand that the universe was created by the word of God, so that what is seen was not made out of things that are visible. *Hebrews 11:3*

The First Article of the Apostles' Creed and its explanation

17 The First Article—Angels

Invisible but Real

We are all aware of the physical world God created. However, Colossians 1:16 tells us there is more to God's creation than we can see: "For by Him all things were created, in heaven and on earth, visible and invisible."

In the beginning, God created invisible creatures that have been part of His creation ever since. Though God created these invisible creatures called angels as perfect and sinless, by their own choice some rebelled against God and chose to be evil (2 Peter 2:4; sometimes these are called demons or devils). There are, therefore, two very different kinds of angels—good and evil. Though we can see the work of both kinds of angels if we know what to look for, the only information we have about them comes from the Bible.

Angels

First, let's dispel a couple of myths.

Myth: People turn into angels when they die.

Truth: God created angels as separate beings. They are different from every other creature God created, including humans. We do not turn into angels when we die any more than we would turn into any other creature, such as a cat or dolphin. As a matter of fact, we are God's special creatures, created in His own image.

Myth: Angels look like chubby little babies.

Truth: Because angels are unseen, invisible creatures, people have taken artistic license throughout the centuries to show angels as chubby little babies with wings, as feminine figures, or in many other ways.

Now, let's look at the biblical account to see how God Himself describes His angelic creatures. Are they cuddly and soft or powerful warriors? Read the following verses, and describe the work the angels do in each.

1. 2 Kings 19:35

2. Daniel 6:16–22

3. What do the angels do in the following verses? How do the people react to them?
a. Luke 1:26–38

Gabriel announced Jesus' impending birth to Mary. She is told not to be afraid.
b. Luke 2:13–14

A multitude of angels announced the birth of Jesus to the shepherds and sang praises to God for the gift of His peace toward all people. The shepherds were told not to be afraid.

So, what's the verdict? We don't know exactly what angels look like because they are spirits who can at times appear in various forms. But we do know that God's angels are fierce warriors, strong and mighty, who at their very presence must reassure the people they greet not to be afraid. They are strong protectors of God's people. What a comfort to know that the angels who served God and His people so effectively in the past are still alive and well and ready to serve us! Think about the following promises of God about angels and also about the Bible references above. Then answer the questions that follow.

Are they not all ministering spirits sent out to serve for the sake of those who are to inherit salvation? (Hebrews 1:14)

For He will command His angels concerning you to guard you in all your ways. On their hands they will bear you up, lest you strike your foot against a stone (Psalm 91:11–12).

1. Why does God send His angels among us?

2. How can we be sure there will be enough angels to go around?

3. How can we be sure angels will be powerful enough to help?

To Review and Remember

For He will command His angels concerning you to guard you in all your ways. On their hands they will bear you up, lest you strike your foot against a stone. *Psalm 91:11–12*

Are they not all ministering spirits sent out to serve for the sake of those who are to inherit salvation? *Hebrews 1:14*

Be sober-minded; be watchful. Your adversary the devil prowls around like a roaring lion, seeking someone to devour. Resist him, firm in your faith, knowing that the same kinds of suffering are being experienced by your brotherhood throughout the world. *1 Peter 5:8–9*

The First Article and its explanation

18 The First Article—Humanity

The Crown of Creation

Imagine the world as God created it before there were humans. It was perfect in every detail, covered with beautiful and useful plants, ready to be cultivated and used. Think of the beauty and variety of animals, birds, and fish, all perfect, none diseased or damaged. How could God create something even better than all this? In what ways was the creation of humans special? What makes humanity the *crown* of God's creation?

To find out, check the Bible references and answer the questions.

1. How did God create other creatures? See Genesis 1:20–22, 24–25.

2. How did God create humans? See Genesis 2:7, 21–22.

3. What relationship does man have to other living things? See Genesis 1:26.

4. What makes humans especially close to God? See Genesis 1:26–27.

What Do We Do Now?

God made the first man and woman to be more than only "takers," creatures who take from creation and give nothing in return. The newly married Adam and Eve were given serious responsibilities within God's creation. In Genesis 1:28, God gave them three general responsibilities. Explain in your own words what they were.

1.

2.

3.

In an earlier lesson, we learned that Adam and Eve sinned and lost the image of God—their holiness—and destroyed the perfection of God's creation. They were forced to leave Eden, and their lives were cursed by sin. Their work was no longer the perfect joy it had been in Paradise. The children that would be born to their marriage would sometimes bring them sorrow. Innocence was lost; death would follow. Yet God promised a Savior to crush sin's hold (Genesis 3:15).

It is important to understand the difference in worldview between what the Bible teaches about people and what different philosophies teach. For example, evolutionists believe that man and woman are not the "crown of creation" but rather have evolved from apelike beings. So, on the one hand, we have the Bible, which teaches that God Himself placed His image on man and woman and shaped us out of the clay of the earth. On the other hand, evolution claims that we are all here because of a gigantic accident. The truth is that no one but God was there to witness the origin of the universe or the origin of life. So, we hold to the biblical account, trusting that by faith, we can know and rely on God, who made us as His "crown of creation."

God Made Me Who I Am

Not only did God create the first man and woman, but He is also still at work granting the miracle of life to so many each day. The infinite variety of characteristics that distinguish us one from another (or, in the case of identical twins, that make us alike) is nothing short of miraculous! Each of us has a unique combination of characteristics, talents, and circumstances.

1. List three special talents God has given you.

2. List three weaknesses or limitations you think you have.

"Each has his own gift from God, one of one kind and one of another" (1 Corinthians 7:7). How are you using—or how might you use—your talents to thank God and to help people? How is one of your weaknesses also a blessing to you or others (2 Corinthians 12:9–10)?

Since we have such great gifts from God, including the gift of a Savior from sin, we can respond with thanksgiving. In the following space, write a brief prayer of thanksgiving for what you are and what you have by God's grace.

To Review and Remember

The Lord God formed the man of dust from the ground and breathed into his nostrils the breath of life, and the man became a living creature. *Genesis 2:7*

For You formed my inward parts; You knitted me together in my mother's womb. *Psalm 139:13*

Before I formed you in the womb I knew you. *Jeremiah 1:5*

The First Article and its explanation

41

19 The First Article—God Takes Care of Me

"God Helps Those Who . . ."

Have you ever heard the phrase "God helps those who help themselves"? Where do you think this phase came from? If your answer is the Bible, you're wrong. Many attribute the quote to Benjamin Franklin, who included it in his *Poor Richard's Almanac*; however, it actually came from a 1698 article by Algernon Sydney. Why does this matter?

It matters because actually the opposite is true! Yes, God wants us to work and take care of our lives and do all the things that we can to provide for those around us. But the truth is that **God helps those who *can't* help themselves**, which includes all of us. God provides not only everything we need spiritually, including salvation and eternal life, but it is also from His hand that everything comes to us—food, house, clothing, home, and family. In this lesson, we will discuss how God uses many ways to preserve His people and His creation.

By God's Direct Blessings

Think of some ways God provides for our needs directly, ways in which man could not substitute anything to replace God's mighty work. The Bible references will help you think of examples.

Matthew 5:45

Job 12:10

Mark 4:41

By Our Own Hard Work

God also protects and preserves us by giving us the ability to work diligently and plan wisely. Even when the Lord God rained manna from heaven for the Israelites to make into bread, He still expected them to gather and prepare it (Exodus 16:4–5; Numbers 11:7–8). By this example, He made clear

His intent to preserve people, in part, by enabling them to work and plan.

Jesus later warned, in one of His parables, of the danger of taking personal credit for God's work of preservation. Read Luke 12:16–21 and answer the following questions.

1. How did the rich man happen to have an extra large crop?

2. What was wrong with his plan to build bigger barns?

3. Why do you think God ended his life?

4. How might the rich man have pleased God with his crops?

By Those Who Love Us

We can see God's special care for us through others when we are either very young, very sick, badly injured, or very old—times when we can't take care of ourselves. But even when we are old enough or young enough or well enough to take care of ourselves, God blesses us through people who love us. Tell about the blessings God gives through loved ones.

The eyes of all look to You, and You give them their food in due season.

Psalm 145:15

By Those All around Us

Brainstorm with your class to think about how God provides for us in the smallest way. Take the examples shown and describe who makes these things happen.

You buy a loaf of bread at the store. What was the process it took, and who was responsible for bringing it there?

Your pharmacist gives you medicine for your ear infection. Who made that happen?

A speeding car gets pulled over by the local police. Who protected you?

These are examples of the teaching of *vocation*, that God works through people to accomplish all good things for us. Each one of us also, as we fulfill our vocations, work together to serve God and our neighbor. As a sister, you might help your sibling with homework. As a son, you might help unload the dishwasher to help your family. As a student, you do your homework to learn and grow in wisdom. What are some things that you do to fulfill your various vocations?

What about Sickness, Trouble, and Death?

In times of trouble, people sometimes ask, "What did I ever do to deserve this? Where was God when I really needed Him?"

Read Romans 8:28–39. Then answer these questions.

1. What are some troubles even Christians have?

2. How can we *know* that "for those who love God *all things* work together for good" (v. 28, emphasis added)?

3. Which of these verses means the most to you? Why?

To Review and Remember

Man and beast You save, O LORD. *Psalm 36:6*

We know that for those who love God all things work together for good, for those who are called according to His purpose. *Romans 8:28*

As a father has compassion on his children, so the LORD shows compassion to those who fear Him. *Psalm 103:13*

The First Article and its explanation

20 The Second Article—Jesus Christ: True God

Who Is Jesus?

Who Jesus is remains an eternally important question for each of us. It is far too important to be answered by rumor, public opinion, or our own theories. God's Word is the only fully trustworthy source of information about the true identity of Jesus.

Why is He called Jesus Christ?

a. Read Matthew 1:21. From this verse, what does the name *Jesus* mean?

b. The title "Christ" means "the anointed." Read Acts 10:38 and summarize below.

Jesus Is Called God

The Bible shows that Jesus is *true God* by calling Him names used only for God. After each Bible reference, write the name of God that Jesus is called.

1.1 John 5:20

2. Matthew 16:16

3. John 20:28

4. Matthew 17:5

1. John 1:1–3

2. Matthew 28:20b

3. Hebrews 13:8

4. John 21:17

The Description Fits Only God

Besides calling Jesus by divine names, the Bible describes Him in ways that can describe only God. Tell in your own words how the following references describe Jesus as God.

Know Him by His Acts

Jesus, true man, did things that only God can do. Select one or more of the following references, and read it carefully. Then, answer the questions. If others report on references you did not choose, fill in that information as well.

1. The healing of the paralytic (Mark 2:1–12)
a. What was Jesus doing when the men brought the paralytic to Him?

b. Why did Jesus' statement in verse 5 anger the scribes?

c. What two things did Jesus do that show He is God?

2. The stilling of the storm (Mark 4:35–41)
a. How do you know the storm was severe?

b. How did Jesus' action show that He is God?

c. What led the disciples to say what they did in verse 41?

3. The raising of Lazarus (John 11:38–44)
a. Why do you think Jesus delayed His coming until Lazarus was dead (vv. 15, 40, 42, 45)?

b. What did He do that only God could do?

c. What even greater miracle did the raising of Lazarus foreshadow (Matthew 28:7)?

Jesus Came for Me

Only by living among us as true man could Jesus fulfill God's Law for us. Only by the sacrifice of the holy, innocent Son of God would the price be high enough to pay for all the sins of humankind. Only God could love us enough to work out such a wonderful plan. What do *you* think of Jesus?

The Second Article—Redemption

And in Jesus Christ, His only Son, our Lord, who was conceived by the Holy Spirit, born of the Virgin Mary, suffered under Pontius Pilate, was crucified, died and was buried. He descended into hell. The third day He rose again from the dead. He ascended into heaven and sits at the right hand of God, the Father Almighty. From thence He will come to judge the living and the dead.

What does this mean?

I believe that Jesus Christ, true God, begotten of the Father from eternity, and also true man, born of the Virgin Mary, is my Lord, who has redeemed me, a lost and condemned person, purchased and won me from all sins, from death, and from the power of the devil; not with gold or silver, but with His holy, precious blood and with His innocent suffering and death, that I may be His own and live under Him in His kingdom and serve Him in everlasting righteousness, innocence, and blessedness, just as He is risen from the dead, lives and reigns to all eternity. This is most certainly true.

To Review and Remember

For in Him the whole fullness of deity dwells bodily. *Colossians 2:9*

And the Word became flesh and dwelt among us, and we have seen His glory, glory as of the Only Son from the Father, full of grace and truth. *John 1:14*

The blood of Jesus His Son cleanses us from all sin. *1 John 1:7*

The Second Article and its explanation

21 The Second Article—Jesus Christ: True Man

Jesus, True Man

Olivia had reluctantly agreed to play the part of Mary in the Christmas program yet again this year. She was already thirteen. Why couldn't they ever have anyone else do it? Still, even though she was grumbling, she went to the rehearsals, learned her short lines, and wore the old sheet that was cut into a robe. She adjusted her headpiece once more before she reached out to take the baby from his mom. Little Luke, who was only two months old, would be playing baby Jesus this year. Olivia always thought it was kind of cool that in her church they used a real baby instead of a doll in their Christmas pageant.

As the other Sunday School kids gathered around her and sang their last song, Olivia looked down at little Luke. She imagined that this was maybe a little glimpse into what Mary experienced—holding a baby was unfamiliar to Olivia, just like it maybe had been for Mary. But as she looked down at him, she noticed his little fingers, his little eyelashes, and his rosy cheeks, and she wondered what Mary must have thought. Then it struck her. "Wow," Olivia thought, "Jesus really did become one of us, a little baby, to save us."

What is the penalty for sin? (Romans 6:23)

Why did Jesus pay the penalty for our sin? (2 Corinthians 5:21)

Was Jesus Really Human?

Was Jesus really human—just like us? Or did He just look and act human, like a man from Mars in disguise? Check out these references below. Write what human activity or trait each reports.

1. Luke 2:7

2. Mark 3:5

3. Mark 4:38

4. Mark 11:12

5. John 11:35

6. John 19:28

7. Mark 15:37

So you see, Jesus was no make-believe human. He was a real man with real human experiences. Yet He was different in one important way. In 1 Peter 2:22–23, we read: "He [Jesus] committed no sin, neither was deceit found in His mouth. When . . . He suffered, He did not threaten, but continued entrusting Himself to Him who judges justly."

Why Did He Do It?

Why was it necessary for Jesus to be born, to live sinlessly as a true human being, and finally to die as a common criminal? Read each Bible reference below. Then complete the statement beside it with a truth about God and about people that lies behind God's plan to send His only Son into the world.

1. Matthew 5:48: God's Law requires . . .

2. Ecclesiastes 7:20: No man except Jesus . . .

3. Romans 6:23: God's justice requires that . . .

4. John 3:16: Because of His great love, God . . .

5. Galatians 4:4–5: God sent Jesus to . . .

6. Hebrews 2:14: God sent Jesus to . . .

For Me

Perhaps the most amazing aspect of Jesus, God becoming man, is the fact that He did it "for me." Each Christian can say with confidence, "Jesus died for me." The penalty for sin and the power for new life in Christ is yours. Write a prayer below, using the opening, which has been started for you.

Dear Jesus, thank You for coming to rescue me, to save me from my sins. I know that if You hadn't been a true man, You could not have died for me, thus redeeming me from sin, death, and the devil. Today, I especially thank You for . . .

_____

_____

In Your name I pray. Amen.

To Review and Remember

There is one God, and there is one mediator between God and men, the man Christ Jesus. *1 Timothy 2:5*

When the fullness of time had come, God sent forth His Son, born of a woman, born under the law, to redeem those who were under the law, so that we might receive adoption as sons. *Galatians 4:4–5*

The Second Article and its explanation

22 The Second Article—Promises Fulfilled in Christ

God's Timing Was Right

God first promised a Savior to Eve and Adam in the Garden of Eden to give them hope after they disobeyed Him. He repeated His promise of a Savior over and over. He kept that promise at the right time by sending Jesus to be born and to die for the sins of the whole world.

In the box below, match up the Old Testament prophecy and its New Testament fulfillment concerning the birth of Jesus. See Micah 5:2; Isaiah 7:14; Jeremiah 23:5–6; Matthew 2:1; Matthew 1:1, 17; Matthew 1:20–23.

PROPHECY	THE DETAILS	FULFILLMENT
	Descendant of David	
	Virgin birth	
	Born in Bethlehem	

The longest, most beautiful, most detailed prophecy in the Old Testament for which we have a New Testament parallel is in Isaiah 53:2–12. Remember that Isaiah wrote these inspired words some seven hundred years before Jesus was born.

Read the five prophecies from Isaiah. Then, in the box, write how each was fulfilled in John 19–20.

PROPHECY	THE DETAILS	FULFILLMENT
Isaiah 53:4		John 19:1–3
Isaiah 53:7		John 19:8–9
Isaiah 53:9		John 19:38–42
Isaiah 53:11		John 20:1, 18

Perfect Timing!

Read Galatians 4:4–5. At just the right time—God's time—God kept His promise made to Adam and Eve and to all people: to send a Savior, Jesus, who would be the hope and salvation for all sinners. God's decision to fulfill His promise was deliberate. He waited until "the fullness of time."

Unscramble the following sentences to learn what conditions at the time of Jesus' birth made the time right for this greatest event in all history.

1. language became the Greek universal first

2. order world nations The among the of government kept Roman the

3. roads travel made Roman easier

4. throughout The people nations Jewish the scattered were

Who Is Jesus?

What a surprise it must have been for people of Jesus' day to realize who He was—the promised Savior!

Pretend that you are a newspaper or TV reporter during Jesus' lifetime, asking a number of people the question "Who is Jesus?" Write or record a report of your findings. Start with these names and references: the shepherds (Luke 2:15–18); Jesus (Mark 14:61–62); Peter (Matthew 16:16); Mary, Jesus' mother (Luke 1:35). Add others from Scripture. Use a computer template to create a "front page" of your paper.

The Savior Jesus—God's Promise for You

Because God kept His Old Testament promises of a Savior, we can trust that He will keep all His promises to us *at the right time*—the time He knows is best for us.

Reread the Second Article. On a sheet of paper, do one of these: Write a personal note that tells why God's promises are important to you. Write a letter to a friend, telling what Jesus did for you when He died and rose again. Write a prayer of praise and thanksgiving for Jesus, your Savior.

To Review and Remember

Call upon Me in the day of trouble; I will deliver you, and you shall glorify Me. *Psalm 50:15*

Behold, I am with you always, to the end of the age. *Matthew 28:20*

Be faithful unto death, and I will give you the crown of life. *Revelation 2:10*

23 The Second Article— Jesus: Our Prophet, Priest, and King

What Do You Do?

Have you ever noticed that when adults meet, the first question they usually ask is "What do you do?" They mean "What kind of work do you do?" Imagine Jesus in the middle of a crowd of people as He arrived in a town. How do you think Jesus would have answered this question?

The name *Christ* means that Jesus was chosen or appointed by God the Father for His work. *Christ* is a Greek word that means "Anointed One." To *anoint* means to pour something like olive oil on a person's head in a solemn ceremony. In ancient times, people were anointed to show that they were chosen for a special job or appointed to a special position. (See 1 Samuel 9 and 16.)

Jesus is the Christ, the Anointed One whom God the Father chose. God chose His Son, Jesus, to do three special kinds of work that people were anointed to do in the Old Testament—the work of Prophet, Priest, and King.

Jesus, Our Prophet

The word *prophet* from a biblical viewpoint means "one who reveals messages from God." How does that meaning fit Jesus? See Acts 10:36 and Mark 1:21–22.

What message did Jesus reveal in His teachings and in His death and resurrection—a message found nowhere else? See Acts 4:12; John 6:68; and *LSB*, p. 156.

Jesus, Our Priest

When we study the Ten Commandments, we learn that God is serious about sin and cannot excuse it. Yet God our Father is merciful and does not want to see His people die forever. How can He punish sin and yet *forgive* the sinner? Someone else must die for the sinner—this is God's plan.

In the Old Testament, priests killed animals and burned them on stone altars. They carried bowls of blood to sprinkle in a room of the temple called the Holy Place. The sacrifices and the blood foreshadowed the coming of the Lamb of God, the great sacrifice for the sins of all people. Jesus, the Lamb of God, would die for all sinners.

Jesus is the Priest like no other priest. Read Hebrews 7:26–28 and 9:12 to find the important difference.

1. How often did Jesus need to shed His blood? Why?

2. What does Jesus do for us as our Priest today? Read Hebrews 7:25 and 1 John 2:1.

Jesus, Our King

The people's highest expectation of Jesus was that He be a great king. Many expected an earthly king. Jesus was much more.

1. What three kingdoms does Jesus rule over? See Catechism Question 125, part C.

2. How is an earthly king's reign different from the actions taken upon Himself by Jesus Christ toward His kingdoms?

To Review and Remember

Lord, to whom shall we go? You have the words of eternal life, and we have believed, and have come to know, that You are the Holy One of God. *John 6:68–69*

He is the propitiation for our sins, and not for ours only but also for the sins of the whole world. *1 John 2:2*

The Second Article and its explanation

24 The Second Article—Christ Died for Us

When Things Go Wrong

"God, why can't I do anything right?" Chelsea prayed as she threw herself onto her bed. "Why do all these bad things happen to me?"

Chelsea had failed an algebra test, and so her dad had grounded her for two weeks. She wasn't allowed to play in the volleyball match after school because her coach said she had a "bad attitude" at practice. Chelsea totally ignored her best friend, Jessi, when Jessi came to school wearing the same jeans Chelsea had been saving her money to buy.

Chelsea wondered what else could go wrong in her life.

What Sin Does

When we sin—or when someone sins against us—we get a hint of God's feelings toward sin and sinners. We often hurt people or are hurt by selfishness, greed, and disobedience. How does God feel about sin? What does our sin do to our relationship with God? Find out in Isaiah 59:2 and Deuteronomy 27:26, and write your answers.

So what!? So what if our sin makes God angry with us and separates us from Him? We'll get along just fine on our own, right? But we can't get along without God. He is our Creator, the One who knows us more intimately than anyone could possibly know us. We need to be brought back together with God. What do these Bible verses tell us about the "wages of our sin" and the result that sin has on our relationship with God? Read Luke 15:11–16 and Romans 6:23.

God's Plan to Make Things Right

The *bad news* is that we can't make up with God or save ourselves from sin and the devil's power over us. But the *good news* is that God has made up with us. He has *reconciled* us to Himself through the saving actions of His Son, Jesus, our Savior. Read about God's reconciliation for us in 2 Corinthians 5:18–21. Tell in your own words how God made things right for us sinners.

_____ in this: while _____ was still a sinner, Christ died for _____ ."

Through Jesus, we are

RECONCILED

RECONNECTED

REUNITED

REJOINED

RESTORED

And nothing can separate us from the love of God!

What Did Jesus Do?

The *best news* is that Jesus took this burden of sin upon Himself. Sin separated us from God, but Jesus' cross provided the bridge so that God could come to us and forgive us. We don't have to try to "climb up to heaven" through our own good works, our earnest prayers, or our religious efforts. Christ came to us!

Look at three statements below that show Jesus' work on our behalf. Unscramble the words by reading the verses below each statement to figure out what the word refers to:

1. Jesus __ __ __ __ __ a perfect life for us. (DLVIE)
Read 2 Corinthians 8:9 and Matthew 8:20.

2. Jesus __ __ __ __ __ __ __ __ and bore the burden of sin for us. (FEDFRESU)
Read Isaiah 53:3 and Matthew 27:46.

3. Jesus finally gave up His life and __ __ __ __ for us. (IEDD)

Read John 19:30.

By Jesus' most amazing gifts of love and mercy, He has redeemed us to the Father. Sin separated us from God, but Jesus reconciled us, or brought us back to Him. We read about that reconciliation and its cost in the explanation of the Second Article:

[Jesus Christ] has redeemed me, a lost and condemned person, purchased and won me from all sins, from death, and from the power of the devil; not with gold or silver, but with His holy, precious blood and with His innocent suffering and death.

In human terms, what God has done for us is incredible, unbelievable. But God has done just that for each of us. Read Romans 5:8 and put your name in the verse. For example, "God shows His love for

To Review and Remember

And you, who once were alienated and hostile in mind, doing evil deeds, He has now reconciled in His body of flesh by His death, in order to present you holy and blameless and above reproach before Him. *Colossians 1:21–22*

I am sure that neither death nor life, nor angels nor rulers, nor things present nor things to come, nor powers, nor height nor depth, nor anything else in all creation, will be able to separate us from the love of God in Christ Jesus our Lord. *Romans 8:38–39*

The Second Article and its explanation

25 The Second Article—Christ Rose for Us

All of Eternity Hinged on This Moment

There are moments in history when everything changes from that time forward. One of these pivotal events was the invention of the printing press around AD 1440. Another event that changed the world was Luther's posting of the Ninety-five Theses, which sparked a movement known as the Reformation. World wars, inventions, notable people—all of these factors change the course of human history. We also see dramatic changes in society from the last century—the rise of the computer age, the fall of the Berlin wall, the tragedy of 9/11. The list could go on.

However, if there is one moment in all of history to which we could point and afterward say, "Now, nothing will be the same," that one event would be the resurrection of Jesus.

If you have attended church for a number of years and are familiar with the Christian message, the idea that Jesus was raised from the dead may seem like "old news" to you; however, this is news that never gets old. Jesus, who claimed He would raise Himself from the dead, actually fulfilled this pledge. If you have ever seen the dead body of a relative or even of a beloved pet, you know how final and powerful death can be. Life just . . . ends. But not for Jesus. His life, ended by a brutally painful crucifixion, was restored to Him three days later.

And after this moment, nothing will ever be the same.

If you think about the concept of death, one word seems to stick on our minds: *irreversible*.

Victory over Death in Jesus

Read John 14:6 and Psalm 23:4. Tell in your own words what Jesus says about traveling through the valley of the shadow of death. Who is the Shepherd and Guide? Where does the valley lead? How can Jesus be "the way"?

Read 1 Corinthians 15:57. Make this your daily prayer.

Jesus Will Raise Us from the Dead

We can ask our friends what it's like to go to a dance or register for high school. They've been there and can tell us about it. But none of us can know what it's like to die and be buried in the grave. The unknown can be frightening.

But Jesus has been through it all! He suffered, died, and was buried. On the third day, He became alive just as He promised, so that we might be with Him someday. He is "the way" through this life into

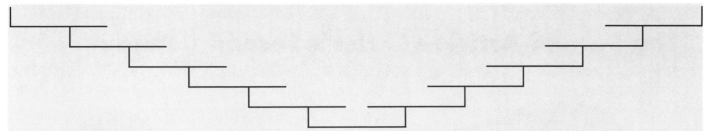

our heavenly life. We can lean on Him. We can trust that He will give us new life.

Read about Jesus giving Lazarus new life in John 11:17–44. Write Jesus' words from verses 25–26 onto a note card and post it where you will see it often.

Jesus' Work of Redemption

The work of Jesus, both true God and true man, can be divided into two parts: the state (or condition) of humiliation and the state of exaltation. See Catechism Questions 127 and 141.

Jesus always had the full powers of God, but in the state of humiliation, He didn't always or fully *use* these divine powers. (In Matthew 2:13; Luke 4:29; and Mark 15, you can see where He didn't; in Mark 4:35–41; Mark 9:2–10; and John 18:1–6, you can see where He did use divine power.)

In the state of exaltation, Jesus, according to His human nature, always and fully uses the divine attributes (the power and glory He has as God) communicated to His human nature. Jesus today continues in His state of exaltation.

Read Philippians 2:6–11. The first three verses of this section describe Jesus' state of humiliation. The next three verses describe His state of exaltation.

On each step of the above diagram of the two states of Christ's work of salvation, write++ one action from the Apostles' Creed: "in Jesus Christ, His only Son, our Lord, who was . . ."

Jesus Is Victorious!

Read 1 Peter 3:18–19; Colossians 2:15; and Catechism Question 143. Why did Jesus descend into hell? Why is Jesus' descent into hell part of His state of exaltation rather than His state of humiliation?

Read Catechism Question 145, and complete the following sentence. Christ's resurrection gives us certainty and proof of the following:

a.

b.

c.

d.

What comfort and assurance do you feel, knowing and believing that Jesus died and rose again, knowing and believing that Jesus is guiding you through the "valley of the shadow of death" as you live each day?

To Review and Remember

[Jesus said,] "I am the resurrection and the life. Whoever believes in Me, though he die, yet shall he live, and everyone who lives and believes in Me shall never die." *John 11:25–26*

Because I live, you also will live. *John 14:19*

Thanks be to God, who gives us the victory through our Lord Jesus Christ. *1 Corinthians 15:57*

The Second Article and its explanation

55

26 The Second Article—Christ's Second Coming

Don't Worry—I'll Be Back!

"Don't worry, I'll be back! Then I'll take you with me," Dad promised before he drove away from his family. "Take care of one another, and tell everyone that I am coming back soon." He was leaving to begin a better job in an exciting location and to close the deal on a beautiful, new house for his wife and children. His family waved until Dad turned a street corner and they could no longer see him.

After a month of long days and many phone calls, Dad returned to Chestnut Street and to his family. He was followed by a moving van with workers ready to load their household possessions. He knew his family eagerly anticipated their new life and were ready to join him. Dad ran through the house shouting, "I'm back! I'm back! I'm here to take you with me!"

How do you think the family felt when Dad came back to take them to their new home?

In a small group or with a partner, tell about a time when someone promised you, "I'll be back." How did you feel? Were you worried? Did that person keep his or her promise and return? What happened then?

Jesus Promised to Return

Jesus also promised to come back to His followers and friends. After He rose from the dead, Jesus appeared to His disciples many times and in spectacular ways. After His resurrection, what promise and command did Jesus give to His first disciples and to us? See Matthew 28:19–20.

Jesus' promise:

Jesus' command:

When Jesus ascended into heaven, the disciples didn't want to lose sight of their Friend and Savior, and they kept looking up. Read Acts 1:1–11. Write the promise the angels gave to Jesus' followers.

Which promise was more certain to be kept—Jesus' promise or Dad's promise to return? Why?

Come, Lord Jesus!

Just as Dad's family probably expected to see him come back for them any day or night, the Early Christian Church expected Jesus to return within a short time of His ascending into heaven. Dad may have phoned, e-mailed, or texted his family to tell them what time he would be back on Chestnut Street so his wife and children could watch for him. But God's timing is not known, and Jesus' return is not predictable. We will receive no advance notice.

1. What does Jesus tell His followers in Acts 1:7 about the time of His return?

2. The Last Day—Judgment Day, when Jesus comes back to earth for the final time—will be like no other day. Read the Bible verses included with Catechism Question 149, part A. In your own words, describe what we know about the day when Jesus returns.

The description of the Last Day and the thought of judgment can seem amazing, awesome, and even frightening. But for Christians, it will be a time of joy. Read Catechism Question 149, part E, and the accompanying Bible verses. Tell why it will be a time of joy for you.

To Review and Remember

Christ, having been offered once to bear the sins of many, will appear a second time, not to deal with sin but to save those who are eagerly waiting for Him. *Hebrews 9:28*

Waiting for our blessed hope, the appearing of the glory of our great God and Savior Jesus Christ. *Titus 2:13*

The Second Article and its explanation

27 The Third Article—The Holy Spirit

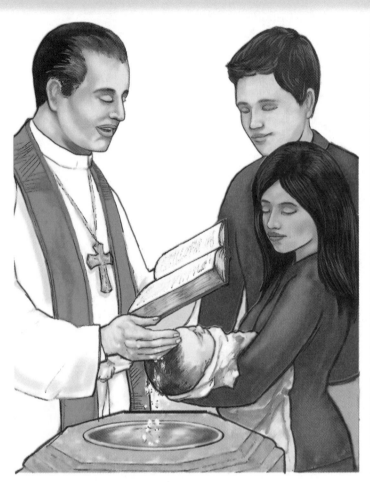

The Third Article—Sanctification

I believe in the Holy Spirit, the holy Christian Church, the communion of saints, the forgiveness of sins, the resurrection of the body, and the life everlasting. Amen.

What does this mean?

I believe that I cannot by my own reason or strength believe in Jesus Christ, my Lord, or come to Him; but the Holy Spirit has called me by the Gospel, enlightened me with His gifts, sanctified and kept me in the true faith.

In the same way He calls, gathers, enlightens, and sanctifies the whole Christian Church on earth, and keeps it with Jesus Christ in the one true faith.

In this Christian Church He daily and richly forgives all my sins and the sins of all believers.

On the Last Day He will raise me and all the dead, and give eternal life to me and all believers in Christ.

This is most certainly true.

God: Father, Son, and Holy Spirit

As you learned in Lessons 15 and 20, the teaching of the Holy Trinity is the main confession of the Creeds. There are three persons of the Trinity—Father, Son, and Holy Spirit—but only one God.

The Third Person of the Trinity is the Holy Spirit, who brings us to faith, points us to Jesus, and makes us holy. The Holy Spirit is not merely "energy" or a "force" or "power," but is true God, equal with the Father and the Son.

Why Do We Need the Holy Spirit?

Let's start with who *you* are. What is your natural condition? See Catechism Question 157.

With that in mind, we realize that on our own, we are enemies of God. We do not want to believe in God, nor can we. The Holy Spirit's work is to point us to our Savior and to give us the faith to believe in Him.

The Work of the Spirit

Bringing us to faith and life as God's child requires the work of the Holy Spirit. That work can be described in four parts.

I. HE CALLS US

The Holy Spirit first works in us to invite us or draw us to the Lord. Without the Spirit, we would not know Christ. His saving work would be hidden to us. But the Holy Spirit points to Christ's redemptive work by calling us by the Gospel—the Good News of what God has done through Christ Jesus to forgive and save us.

How did the Holy Spirit call you to faith in Christ? Perhaps the Holy Spirit made you God's child when your parents brought you to Baptism as a baby. Perhaps you came to church as an older child and received the gracious gifts of God through listening to God's Word and later through Baptism. Or perhaps you know that you are God's child, but you still haven't been baptized with water and God's Word. Whatever your situation, write in your own words how God called you to believe in Him and what it means to you.

Even if we do not remember the point in time when the Spirit called us because we were too young, we take comfort in the truth that it is the Spirit's work that made us holy. We didn't have to make a decision or ask God to come to us. As Luther said, a Christian's attitude is that of opening our hands, ready to receive all of the good gifts of God and thank Him for them.

II. HE ENLIGHTENS US

The Holy Spirit not only brings us to faith through the Gospel, but He also helps us to understand that Gospel.

How does the Holy Spirit do this? Read the following verses and summarize.

1. John 14:26

2. John 16:13

The Holy Spirit always points us to Jesus—He gives us "enlightenment," or understanding, so that we can understand the Gospel, or God's Good News for us.

III. HE SANCTIFIES US

The word *sanctifies* means "to be made holy." How does the Holy Spirit do this? The Holy Spirit makes us holy by bringing us to the Lord. This work of sanctification cannot be done by our efforts; rather, the Holy Spirit *makes* us holy. Me, holy? You, holy? Yes—by the power of God!

Because our sins are removed and we are guilt-free, we can do good works. We do good works not to earn heaven (we can't earn it; Jesus did it for us), not because we are such good people (that sounds like pride and self-righteousness). As God's people, we do good works for His glory. This is what He wants in our lives (Ephesians 2:10; Matthew 5:16).

Through the power of the Holy Spirit, and to give glory to God,

what good works can you do at home?

what good works can you do for your friends?

what good works do you do that show others what it means to be a Christian?

IV. HE KEEPS US

What a comfort and relief it is to know that God works to keep us in faith and to keep us as His people.

James 4:7: The Holy Spirit even helps us to **resist the devil.**

Romans 8:26: The Holy Spirit even helps us to **pray.**

To Review and Remember

By grace you have been saved through faith. And this is not your own doing; it is the gift of God, not a result of works, so that no one may boast. For we are His workmanship, created in Christ Jesus for good works. *Ephesians 2:8–10*

The Third Article and its explanation

28 The Third Article—The Holy Christian Church

Where's Your Church?

Imagine a group of people from your church eating dinner together at a restaurant. As they discuss an upcoming event, the waiter asks, "Where is your church?" Everyone quickly and automatically points toward the southwest corner of the restaurant. "Right down the highway, that way," they reply.

If someone asked you where your church was, what would you answer?

Jesus promises, "For where two or three are gathered in My name, there am I among them" (Matthew 18:20). Now, where would you say your church is?

I Believe in the Holy Christian Church

The Holy Spirit and the Holy Christian Church are mentioned side by side in the Apostles' Creed because they have an important relationship with each other. I confess that the Holy Spirit not only makes me holy—keeps *me* growing in true faith—

but also makes *all* Christians holy and keeps the *whole* community of believers in the true faith. Why do we call the Holy Christian Church "the communion of saints"?

The Invisible and Visible Christian Church

Picture yourself driving by a construction site every day at which many workers are building a church sanctuary. Each day, you notice their progress. The foundation is poured. Wall studs, floor joists, and ceiling rafters get bolted and nailed securely. Beautiful stained glass windows are installed. The masons secure one brick at a time. And at last they have finished the *building*.

But this structure provides only a place of worship and learning for the real Christian Church—the people. The steeple, the landscaping, the doors, the skylights, the altar, and the cross—these all add to a worship-filled atmosphere. But without Spirit-filled people, the building itself would be only an empty shell, a number on a street.

The Holy Christian Church is *invisible* because we cannot see one's faith in Jesus, which is what makes people members of the Church. How, then, can we know if we belong? How can we know who else belongs? Read 1 Peter 2:9–10.

The Holy Christian Church is visible in that we can look around us and see and hear others confessing the same saving faith in Jesus Christ that we confess. These people are the visible church. What do we have in common with other believers?

There Am I among Them

Jesus clearly wants us to join others who confess their Christian faith and read and study the Word of God. When we meet with other Christians regularly for worship, we form a congregation. The individual congregations of St. Mark's Lutheran Church, St. Timothy Lutheran Church, Our Savior Lutheran Church, and New Hope Lutheran Church, for example, unite with other congregations that teach the same doctrine to form a denomination. What is the name of your church congregation? your church denomination? What other denominations can you name?

Being a Christian in the visible Church may be confusing. Since there are so many denominations and congregations in the world, how can we know and support the true visible Church? Read each Bible reference and write a short guideline in question form to help you evaluate the teachings of a visible church body.

1 Timothy 6:3

Romans 16:17–18

Matthew 28:19–20

Pray that God may help us hold firmly to His truth, and pray that He will bless His Church on earth.

To Review and Remember

Where two or three are gathered in My name, there am I among them. *Matthew 18:20*

You are a chosen race, a royal priesthood, a holy nation, a people for His own possession, that you may proclaim the excellencies of Him who called you out of darkness into His marvelous light. *1 Peter 2:9*

The Third Article and its explanation

29 The Third Article—Forgiveness of Sins

The Way God Sees Me

Talk with two or three classmates about these situations.

1. Carla shared a secret with her friend Jenny, but then found out that her secret had been made public. Carla sees Jenny in the hall at school and confronts Jenny, who says . . .
2. Sometimes I lie to my parents or teachers about my grades because I'm tired of getting lectured about my schoolwork. But what usually happens when I do this is . . .
3. Sometimes I ignore the rules of fair play or team sportsmanship. Then, what usually happens is . . .
4. I haven't always been willing to tell God and others when I've done wrong and need their forgiveness. Then, what usually happens is . . .

Now, read this situation and help your small group provide an ending, developing this story into a parable that illustrates God's daily and rich forgiveness of sins.

"Finish your math assignment before you go out to shoot hoops," Mom reminded Kevin as she left to get groceries.

Kevin looked at his math page, but closed his book when he heard Mom drive off. We won't have school tomorrow anyway, *he thought.* A snowstorm is coming through, and the buses won't be able to make their runs. I may as well play basketball with my friends while I can.

Kevin played ball until dark, then went in to eat dinner. Mom asked, "Did you understand your math and finish the assignment okay, Kevin?"

Kevin said, . . .

Justification

Like Kevin, we have often gone our own way, forgetting God and disobeying His good laws. How can we hope for God to keep us as members of His family, His Church?

Read Psalm 130:3–4. Which words mean to "count sins"?

God doesn't keep count of our sins. We can "stand" before Him as His children, despite our sins. Which words in the psalm tell us why?

When God forgives, He completely removes the sin—all is forgotten as it is forgiven. God looks at me and sees me *just as if I'd* never sinned. That's what the word *justified* means. God forgives my sins—He justifies me. He says that I am "just," or "righteous," not because of any good things that I may do, but because of His grace, for Jesus' sake. I receive His forgiveness by believing the Gospel—the Good News of Jesus' suffering and death to pay for all my sins.

The doctrine, or teaching, of justification by grace through faith in Jesus Christ is the most important doctrine of our Christian religion. It is the doctrine that separates the Christian religion from all false religions—those that teach that people are saved by their own good works.

Read Romans 3:20–28. Fill in the missing words in these statements about our Christian faith. Do this with a partner and talk about what each statement means to you.

Through God's Law, we become _____ of sin.

_____ people have sinned and need God's forgiveness.

Have you sinned? Do you need God's forgiveness? Ask Him to forgive you right now. Repent to Him in your prayers. Ask Him to help you to forgive others who have said or done things to hurt you. Confess to those whom you have sinned against. Talk with them or write to them about your thoughts, and ask for their forgiveness.

The _____ from God comes through faith in Jesus Christ to all who _____that Jesus has died and risen for their sins.

Remember your Baptism each day. God has made you His child. He has brought you into His family. Rejoice that the Holy Spirit lives in you and keeps you in the true faith. Say the Apostles' Creed, and emphasize all those words that tell of God's actions, which you so heartily believe!

God the Father gives us His forgiveness freely by His_____.

Think of all the gifts God has given you. Thank Him for His goodness. Especially thank God for His grace. We don't deserve anything, including the forgiveness that He freely gives us.

God presented His Son, Jesus, as a _____ of atonement. Jesus' blood paid for all our sins and redeemed us forever.

Think of what sacrifice means in your life. What do you give to someone or do for someone that takes your time, energy, and love? Then, think of the most awesome sacrifice of all—God the Father offering His Son, Jesus, to die for all people's sins! He did it all for us! He bought us back from the devil so we can someday live with Him forever!

By _____, God's forgiveness becomes ours when we believe that Jesus, our Savior, makes us "right with God" and enables us to live for Him.

When the Spirit gives us faith to believe that God has done all this for us through Jesus, we accept His gracious love and forgiveness. Believers are joined together in the Christian life of loving, serving, and forgiving one another. The Holy Spirit lives in our hearts, reminding us that God has justified us through Jesus' blood.

To Review and Remember

The righteousness of God has been manifested ... through faith in Jesus Christ for all who believe. *Romans 3:21–22*

Bearing with one another and, if one has a complaint against another, forgiving each other; as the Lord has forgiven you, so you must also forgive. *Colossians 3:13*

The Third Article and its explanation

30 The Third Article—Resurrection and Life

It's Your Funeral

Do you ever think about death? What are some of your questions and concerns about dying? See what the Bible says.

> The wages of sin is death. (Romans 6:23)
>
> Death spread to all men because all sinned (Romans 5:12)
>
> You are dust, and to dust you shall return (Genesis 3:19)
>
> Blessed are the dead who die in the Lord (Revelation 14:13)
>
> If we have died with [Christ Jesus], we will also live with Him. (2 Timothy 2:11)

Let's face it. Death is frightening. No one who has died can tell us what it's like to die and be buried. Death is a mysterious part of our future. Just thinking about death or being around someone who is dying might give us uncomfortable feelings. Visiting a funeral home perhaps sends shivers up the spine.

Because of sin, death is how life on earth ends. It's the last act of human life since Adam and Eve sinned in the Garden of Eden.

However, as Christians, we can talk about death and plan our funerals without being morbid, without feeling totally unsure of the future, because we have Jesus' sure promise that He is always with us and that He will raise us from the dead.

In small groups or with a partner, talk about these questions:

What would you like your funeral to be like? What songs and Scripture readings would share your faith with the people who attend?

What do you think happens to your earthly body when you die? Where might you want your body to be buried?

What message do you want engraved on your grave marker? How can the message be a witness of your faith to the people who see it?

It's Your Resurrection

One of the truths we confess in the Third Article is "I believe in the . . . resurrection of the body." Whatever sin and death do to our bodies, the Holy Spirit can undo! He is able and willing. As you read and talk about these Bible verses, remember that the temporary ending for our earthly bodies is an eternal beginning for our life in heaven with Jesus.

Why can Christians trust that Jesus will keep His promises? See John 11:23–26.

When will the resurrection of the body take place? See 1 Corinthians 15:20–26, 52.

What will Christ do to the bodies of all believers? See Philippians 3:21.

Read Catechism Questions 187–92 to discover more about resurrection and the Last Day. Based on Scripture, what do you think your resurrection will be like?

Put your Christian faith into actions and words. You've known this family all your life, and you have shared with them a deep faith in Jesus. What would your actions be?

What words could you say to comfort your friend's parents?

Waiting Confidently, Sharing the Hope

While we live our lives each day in the meantime, waiting for our death and resurrection, what do we do? The apostle Paul seemed to be thinking about that question when he wrote: "Therefore, my beloved brothers, be steadfast, immovable, always abounding in the work of the Lord, knowing that in the Lord your labor is not in vain" (1 Corinthians 15:58).

How would your words and actions be different if this family had not known Jesus as their Savior?

1. In the meantime, as you look confidently to your own resurrection, how can you work for the Lord while you live on the earth? Write your ideas here.

2. Imagine that your best friend just died from injuries she received in a car accident. Your parents take you to your friend's home to be with her grieving parents. They cry and ask, "I can't believe we'll never have our daughter with us again. Why did she have to die?"

To Review and Remember

[Jesus said,] "I am the resurrection and the life. Whoever believes in Me, though he die, yet shall he live, and everyone who lives and believes in Me shall never die." *John 11:25–26*

You make known to me the path of life; in Your presence there is fullness of joy; at Your right hand are pleasures forevermore. *Psalm 16:11*

We know that when He appears we shall be like Him, because we shall see Him as He is. *1 John 3:2*

Continue to review the Third Article and its explanation.

31 The Apostles' Creed—This Is Most Certainly True

I Believe

Say the Apostles' Creed to a partner or with a small group of classmates. Look each other in the eye as you declare and proclaim your faith. Remember that the word *creed* comes from the Latin word *credo,* meaning "believe." Christians often say, "This is most certainly true" at the end of a creed to tell God and one another that the words they have said are words from the heart, words by which they live.

Write words and phrases from the Apostles' Creed and the explanations that are particularly meaningful to you.

Jesus promised His first disciples, and He promises you and me, "I am with you always" (Matthew 28:20). He also promises, "Do not be anxious how you are to speak or what you are to say, for what you are to say will be given to you in that hour. For it is not you who speak, but the Spirit of your Father speaking through you" (Matthew 10:19–20).

Jesus, when I hear these promises, I want to say this to You:

Jesus' Words to Us

Jesus plainly spoke about God's redeeming love for all people and about His reason for coming to the earth. He said, "For God so loved the world, that He gave His only Son, that whoever believes in Him should not perish but have eternal life" (John 3:16). After Jesus rose from the dead, He said to His disciples, "Go into all the world and proclaim the gospel to the whole creation. Whoever believes and is baptized will be saved, but whoever does not believe will be condemned" (Mark 16:15–16).

I'm a disciple, Lord. So You must be talking to me too. But, Lord, I want to ask You something:

Put Your Beliefs into Actions

Read these situations with a small group of classmates. Then imagine you are right there in the middle of the conflict. How can you speak, act, and give a witness to your faith? Tell what you might say and do.

1. *Your aunt and uncle have come for a weekend visit. They've brought your cousin Sherry, who is your age. You haven't seen your relatives since you were a toddler, and you're having fun getting to know them.*
   Your parents have taken you and Sherry to a mall to shop today. You've just come out of a department store, and Sherry starts to giggle. She pulls your arm and says, "Hey, cuz, look what I got!" Out of her jacket pocket, she pulls a gold necklace.
   "Where'd you get that?" you blurt out.
   "Just picked it up, cousin, just picked it up!" She winks at you.
   "Sherry! You can't do that! That's stealing."
   "Stealing—schmealing. Come on, what are you? Some kind of goody-goody?"

You look at Sherry and say . . .

You help her to . . .

The situation ends by . . .

2. *A boy named Justin moved into your neighborhood last month. He's quiet and kind of nerdy. He hasn't made any friends at school, but you've talked to him while you walk home together from the bus stop. You like his humbleness and dry sense of humor. You invited Justin to church and Sunday School last week, but he said, "I don't* think I can go. My family's not too religious." *Today you're reading your English assignment in the backyard. You look up, and there's Justin. He looks very tense. "I've got to talk to someone," he says quietly.*
   "What is it, Justin?" you ask.
   And then, in a choked voice, Justin tells you the whole story. His mom went to a business meeting, as she often does on the weekend, and while she was gone, Justin's stepfather shouted at him to clean his room, fold the laundry, and wash the dishes. When Justin didn't get everything done in a short time, his stepfather hit him many times with a broom handle.
   "It's not the first time this has happened," Justin says as he shows you the bruises on his back and legs. "I want it to stop. I might just run away. I don't know what to do."

You look at Justin and say . . .

You help him to . . .

This situation ends by . . .

To Review and Remember

Do not be anxious how you are to speak or what you are to say, for what you are to say will be given to you in that hour. For it is not you who speak, but the Spirit of your Father speaking through you. *Matthew 10:19–20*

You will receive power when the Holy Spirit has come upon you, and you will be My witnesses in Jerusalem and in all Judea and Samaria, and to the end of the earth. *Acts 1:8*

Review the Apostles' Creed and the explanations

32 The Lord's Prayer—Jesus Teaches Us to Pray

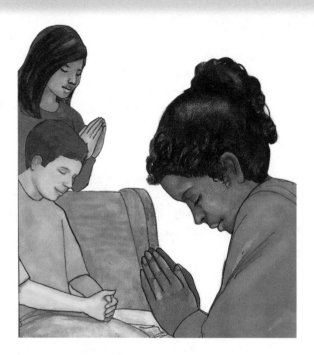

What's Our Heavenly Father Like?

We all know different fathers—our own dad, our best friend's dad, the dad next door. Each one is unique. Some dads are into sports, some into books and movies, while still others may love yard work and gardening. Some dads are strict; some are lenient. Some are loving and attentive; and sadly, others are abusive and cruel. Just like each one of us, our earthly fathers are not perfect, and yet most fathers love their kids and try their best to provide for them. We can draw some similarities between our earthly father and our heavenly Father. Jesus Himself made these comparisons. But even with these similarities, we always have the understanding that the comparison will not be perfect. With all of that in mind, how would you describe the ideal father? What qualities would he have?

Read Catechism Question 205. Consider how you could share the true nature of God with someone who has experienced a poor relationship—or no relationship—with a father.

In Jesus' Name

When Christopher Columbus arrived in the New World, he claimed it for Queen Isabella I of Spain. When Jesus redeemed us, He claimed us for His Father—our Father in heaven. By faith, we now belong to Him. Columbus claimed the new land by the name and under the will of Spain's queen. Jesus invites us to pray in His name and according to God's will.

Read John 14:13–14 and 15:7. Tell in your own words how Jesus invites us to pray to our heavenly Father.

More about Prayer

Use your Bible and catechism to discover more about prayer. Work with a partner or a small group of classmates.

1. Read Psalm 103:8–13. How does our heavenly Father treat us even though we sin against Him each day?

2. Read Catechism Question 195 and, as always, the accompanying Bible texts. To whom should we pray? Why?

3. Read Catechism Question 196. Why is our belief that God is our Father more important to our prayer life than our attempts to do things that please God?

4. What should be included in our prayers? See Catechism Question 197.

5. Describe the three ways we should pray. See Catechism Question 198.

6. How are we helped in our prayer life? Read Romans 8:26–27.

7. Sometimes, God answers our prayers with a fast, resounding "Yes!" Sometimes, His answer is "Wait a while." Other times, He replies, "I have a better idea for you." How can this last answer, a no answer, be the answer to our prayer?

8. Where and when should we pray?

To Review and Remember

See what kind of love the Father has given to us, that we should be called children of God. *1 John 3:1*

The Introduction to the Lord's Prayer

33 The First Petition—God's Holy Name

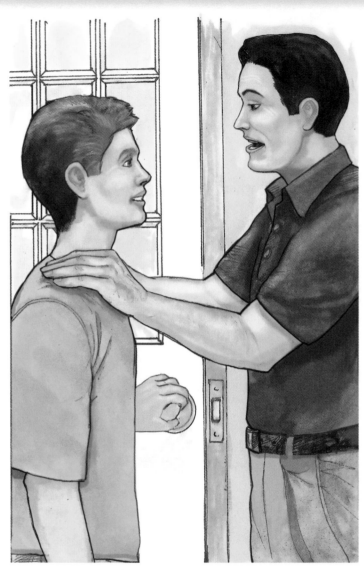

Keeping God's Name Holy

Holy means "set apart for God and worthy of respect." God's name already is holy—designated for Him and deserving honor. We *keep* God's name holy by respecting God and by honoring His name and using it only for His glory. We bring honor to His name as we hear and use His Word and live according to it.

According to Luther's words, nothing we do makes God's name any holier than it already is. Yet we help keep it holy by living according to God's will, by telling others about God, and by using His name in ways that show our respect for Him. This is very similar to the Second Commandment. God's name is already holy; we pray in this petition that we may be able to keep God's name holy in our words and deeds.

We are like the people in the Bible who had the choice to keep God's name holy or to dishonor it by their actions. Like Joshua and the children of Israel, we have the choice to serve the true God or to serve false gods. What are some things that either honor or dishonor God's name? Below are some possibilities for you to consider. Add other actions that you think of as a class.

- Going to church regularly
- Praying that we grow in faith
- Swearing by God's name
- Volunteering to help a neighbor in need
- Wearing a cross around your neck
- Walking away from a group when some of them are swearing
- Ignoring a friend's criticism of the Christian way of life

We want to live God-pleasing lives because God lovingly and graciously gave His only Son for us. Our lives are a *response* to His love. We can never be perfect, but because Jesus died for us and rose again, He has made us "right" with God, and our heavenly Father lovingly forgives and accepts us for Jesus' sake. Read 1 Corinthians 10:23–33. Describe a Christian's motive in your own words.

The First Petition

Hallowed be Thy name.

What does this mean?

God's name is certainly holy in itself, but we pray in this petition that it may be kept holy among us also.

How is God's name kept holy?

God's name is kept holy when the Word of God is taught in its truth and purity, and we, as the children of God, also lead holy lives according to it. Help us to do this, dear Father in heaven! But anyone who teaches or lives contrary to God's Word profanes the name of God among us. Protect us from this, heavenly Father!

c. John 15:12

Give God the Glory

When God called to Moses from the burning bush, He set him apart for a sacred mission. Moses returned to Egypt looking the same as when he left, only older. Yet he was a very different person.

1. God has set you apart for a sacred mission. Though He didn't call to you from a burning bush, God chose you to be His child through an act as miraculous as the burning bush. What action did God take to set you apart for His holy mission? See Romans 6:3–4.

2. What characteristics did God give you at the time He set you apart for His holy mission? Read 1 Peter 2:9–10.

3. By His action in Baptism, God sets us apart to glorify Him. His name is forever upon us, and we are His children, named after Jesus Christ. He leads us to live differently than those who don't know Him as their Lord and Savior. What does God's power through the Holy Spirit help us to do?
a. John 6:40

b. John 15:8

Owning God's Family Name

Even as God's children, we do not always live our lives to His glory. We sin and dishonor the name God gave us through Baptism, but God continues to forgive us repentant sinners and make us holy (set apart) through faith in Jesus Christ. Then the Holy Spirit once again gives us the power to live our lives as His people. He helps us to change and grow, giving us strength to become more Christlike.

Each day before his son left the house to walk to the school bus stop, a father put his hands on his son's shoulders and said, "Remember whose son you are and to what family you belong." What can these words say to us about our relationship to our Lord and our walk through this life?

Show your faith and Jesus' love to others through your Christlike words and actions. What are some ways you can keep God's name holy and live your life to honor Him? Brainstorm ideas with a partner; then pray that the Holy Spirit would help you live according to all that is implied in your name—Christian!

To Review and Remember

Bless the Lord, O my soul, and all that is within me, bless His holy name! *Psalm 103:1*

The First Petition and its explanation

34 The Second Petition—God's Kingdom

The Second Petition

Thy kingdom come.

What does this mean?

The kingdom of God certainly comes by itself without our prayer, but we pray in this petition that it may come to us also.

How does God's kingdom come?

God's kingdom comes when our heavenly Father gives us His Holy Spirit, so that by His grace we believe His holy Word and lead godly lives here in time and there in eternity.

What Is God's Kingdom?

What is a kingdom? Think of a king ruling over his land and people, or his realm. This is, essentially, what a kingdom is, but we don't really think in terms of realms or kingdoms today. Instead, we are more familiar with countries or nations. A kingdom, however, is a place or a people who are ruled by a king. This is the language that the Bible uses to describe God's rule. He is the King—the good King—whose rule extends over all peoples of all countries and nationalities.

So, in this petition, we pray that God's kingdom would come. But what is God's kingdom? God's kingdom is not a landmass, but rather an invisible kingdom of grace, which Christ, as our Savior and Deliverer, rules in all righteousness and mercy.

God's Kingdom Trilogy

A *trilogy* is a series of three parts that are closely related and have the same theme. We frequently find trilogies in musical compositions, movies, and literature series. God's kingdom trilogy is a series of three kingdoms, all related to the work of our triune God.

I. The *kingdom of power* is God's rule over the whole universe—over believers, unbelievers, and all other earthly and heavenly creatures. Christ rules with His omnipotence, omniscience, and omnipresence.

II. The *kingdom of grace* is God's gracious, loving rule through His Word and Sacraments. This kingdom includes only those people who have received God's gift of faith in Christ Jesus. It is the whole Christian Church on earth. God's kingdom comes to us here and now through the kingdom of grace.

III. The *kingdom of glory* includes Christians who have passed from the kingdom of grace into eternity. The angels and the Church in heaven are in Christ's kingdom of glory. God's kingdom will come to us in the return of Christ for all eternity.

This trilogy—the threefold kingdom of God—reveals Christ as King of *all* things. God's kingdom comes to us through the Holy Spirit, who enters our hearts and causes us to believe the Good News. This happens through no actions of our own and without our even praying for it.

For What Do We Pray in the Second Petition?

We do not pray in the Lord's Prayer that God's kingdom of power might come, because it is already present everywhere. So what *do* we pray for? See Catechism Question 213 (and, as always, the accompanying Bible texts). Then restate the answers in your own words.

a.

b.

c.

d.

God's Kingdom of Grace

How can we be sure God's kingdom comes? Our sinful nature would not lead us to this certainty. But God knew our tragic circumstances, and He demonstrated His love for us in His kingdom trilogy. He guarantees that His Means of Grace (His Word and Sacraments) establish and sustain His kingdom.

1. Read Isaiah 55:10–11. What assurance does this word of Scripture give us?

2. How does Jesus affect your life on this earth?

3. God has given His kingdom to us and expects us to tell others about it. We are to do this now. (Note Christ's sense of urgency in John 9:4.) Begin at this moment. Think of people you know who do not have a personal relationship with our Savior. Write a short prayer asking God to open their hearts.

God's Kingdom of Glory

The kingdom of glory is that kingdom Jesus prepares for us in heaven, the kingdom He will give to all who believe in Him, the kingdom to which all believers will belong on the Last Day.

Read Revelation 21:1–4, 10–21. Describe St. John's word picture of our glorious heavenly home.

To Review and Remember

The Lord has established His throne in the heavens, and His kingdom rules over all. *Psalm 103:19*

Jesus answered, "Truly, truly, I say to you, unless one is born of water and the Spirit, he cannot enter the kingdom of God." *John 3:5*

The Lord will rescue me from every evil deed and bring me safely into His heavenly kingdom. *2 Timothy 4:18*

The Second Petition and its explanation

35 The Third Petition—God's Will

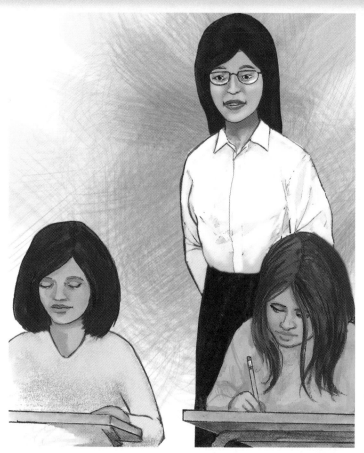

The Third Petition

Thy will be done on earth as it is in heaven.

What does this mean?

The good and gracious will of God is done even without our prayer, but we pray in this petition that it may be done among us also.

How is God's will done?

God's will is done when He breaks and hinders every evil plan and purpose of the devil, the world, and our sinful nature, which do not want us to hallow God's name or let His kingdom come; and when He strengthens and keeps us firm in His Word and faith until we die. This is His good and gracious will.

What Is God's Will?

In the Third Petition, we pray for something that exists even without our prayers. So again, we ask that God would make His will come among us, just as we ask His name to be holy among us and for His kingdom to come to us as well.

Read the first and last chapters of the Book of Job. Many people read this account of Job's faith and think that God should never have allowed Satan to torment Job the way he did. But this Bible story reminds us that God does not send evil into our lives. Suffering, pain, and death are not the result of God's will. Evil comes because Satan and sin exist in this world.

Nevertheless, God remains in control. God keeps evil from going too far. He gives us strength to bear pain and remain faithful to Him. When temptations come our way, He gives us the power to resist. He can bring good to us even within the misfortunes we encounter in this world. And His will to bring us to our perfect, happy, heavenly home will be accomplished.

Discuss with a partner or small group some of the temptations and hardships Satan throws in the path of you and your family. These might be wars, earthquakes, illnesses, forms of abuse, and jealousies. Then discover in God's Word what God's will is for you.

a. Deuteronomy 4:2—It is God's will that we

b. John 6:40—It is God's will that we

c. 1 Timothy 2:4—It is God's will that we

d. 1 Thessalonians 4:3—It is God's will that we

The world, Satan, and our sinful nature are constantly working to pull us away from God's kingdom. But God promises to save and protect us, and through the power of the Spirit, to keep us in His kingdom of grace and (future) glory.

God's Opponents

The evil powers in our world working against God's will are most evident in violent crimes, bloody warfare, and social injustice. These evil powers (see Catechism Question 216) also actively tempt us to do things we know we shouldn't do.

1. Julia's teacher caught her copying a friend's answers onto her homework paper. Julia gave this excuse: "The devil made me do it." What evil power does 1 Peter 5:8 warn us against?

2. Sean's aunt caught him taking a $20 bill from her wallet. Sean retorted, "But I really need it. I don't like my old jacket. I want a new one!" Of what does 1 John 2:15–17 remind us?

3. Stephanie's homeroom teacher reprimanded her and then called her parents because she has been late to school seventeen times this quarter. Stephanie whines, "Yeah, I know. But it's not my fault. I really do try to get here on time. I'm just not a morning person, and I can't get moving any faster." What does Romans 7:18 tell us?

God's Will Accomplished in Your Life

Read again the explanation to the Third Petition. Then read Catechism Question 218. Write in your words how God's will in Christ Jesus is done in your life.

a. Romans 16:20

b. 1 Peter 1:5

c. Psalm 119:35

d. 2 Corinthians 12:9

To Review and Remember

We know that for those who love God all things work together for good, for those who are called according to His purpose. *Romans 8:28*

The Third Petition and its explanation

75

36 The Fourth Petition—God's Gifts

The Fourth Petition

Give us this day our daily bread.

What does this mean?

God certainly gives daily bread to everyone without our prayers, even to all evil people, but we pray in this petition that God would lead us to realize this and to receive our daily bread with thanksgiving.

What is meant by daily bread?

Daily bread includes everything that has to do with the support and needs of the body, such as food, drink, clothing, shoes, house, home, land, animals, money, goods, a devout husband or wife, devout children, devout workers, devout and faithful rulers, good government, good weather, peace, health, self-control, good reputation, good friends, faithful neighbors, and the like.

Our Daily Bread

Read Catechism Questions 219–22. "Daily bread" includes everything we need to live on earth. God wants us both to ask Him for everything we need and to show concern for the needs of others. God desires that we receive His gifts *with*

and *without*

God has given you a great wealth of gifts. List five of the most unusual ones:

1.

2.

3.

4.

5.

Our Gracious God

God provides for our physical needs. (As His redeemed people, we also enjoy great spiritual blessings, particularly grace and forgiveness, which abound daily through Christ.) God's good and gracious blessings to us lead us to respond with contentment, generosity, and thanksgiving.

1. What is God's message to you about being content? See Matthew 6:25–34.

2. God blesses you; what is His will that you now do? See 2 Corinthians 9:8–12.

3. We receive many gifts and blessings—many we didn't ask for or don't appreciate. Write a prayer you might pray with your family tonight. Think about things you are learning in the Fourth Petition of the Lord's Prayer and special reasons you have to thank and praise God.

through our church?

through our family?

individually?

Sharing What We Have

Recall or review the story of Jesus feeding the five thousand (Luke 9:10–17). Suppose Jesus had asked His disciples, "What are you going to do with the twelve baskets of leftovers?" What are some possible answers the disciples might have given?

Think again of the abundance our country enjoys—so much that we throw away tons of unused or worn-out material each day. Yet many in our world have too little and suffer because of it. We are directed to share with those in need.

Look at the example of the Early Christian Church in Acts 4:32–35. Then consider the poor in our world today, both in our own country and throughout the world. How can we help them through our government?

God provides everything we need in this life. It is His will that we thank Him and share our blessings with others. What "daily bread" blessings did you share last week? What specific thing will you do this week to share your blessings?

Better than any of these earthly blessings, however, is the forgiveness and grace shown to us through Christ. Yes, we always thank God for giving us "our daily bread," but how much better is the feast of feasts that He has given us in the Lord's Supper, in which we eat a bread that satisfies eternally. Praise to You, O Christ!

To Review and Remember

Seek first the kingdom of God and His righteousness, and all these things will be added to you. *Matthew 6:33*

So then, as we have opportunity, let us do good to everyone, and especially to those who are of the household of faith. *Galatians 6:10*

37 The Fifth Petition—God's Forgiveness

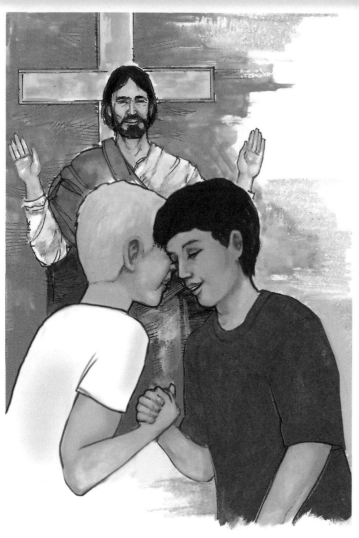

God's Undeserved Forgiveness

When we pray the Fifth Petition, we realize that we are truly lost without God's forgiveness. For we well know that even though God gives us faith through Baptism, and strengthens it as we hear His Word and know and believe the Gospel, we still daily sin and fall short of what God demands. We still live in the world, among people who may irritate us. We have our own sinful flesh always lulling us into laziness, meanness, and greed. And Satan is the expert at attacking us and luring us into disbelief and despair. So, in this petition, we pray for God's forgiveness. God freely and lovingly forgives us. As Luther says in his Large Catechism, "It is not as though He did not forgive sin without and even before our prayer. (He has given us the Gospel, in which is pure forgiveness before we prayed or ever thought about it [Romans 5:8].) But the purpose of this prayer is that we may recognize and receive such forgiveness" (The Lord's Prayer 88).

1. In the Fifth Petition, what do we ask? What do we promise?

2. Why do we ask God to give us everything by *grace?* (Read Psalm 130:3 before you write your answer.)

The Fifth Petition

And forgive us our trespasses as we forgive those who trespass against us.

What does this mean?

We pray in this petition that our Father in heaven would not look at our sins, or deny our prayer because of them. We are neither worthy of the things for which we pray, nor have we deserved them, but we ask that He would give them all to us by grace, for we daily sin much and surely deserve nothing but punishment. So we too will sincerely forgive and gladly do good to those who sin against us.

We Ask for Forgiveness

God desires that we ask Him to forgive our sins. As a matter of fact, many psalms are prayers for forgiveness. Pray these words of Psalm 32:1–5 responsively with your classmates.

Group A: Blessed is the one whose transgression is forgiven, whose sin is covered.

Group B: Blessed is the man against whom the LORD counts no iniquity, and in whose spirit there is no deceit.

Reader 1: For when I kept silent, my bones wasted away through my groaning all day long.

Reader 2: For day and night Your hand was heavy upon me; my strength was dried up as by the heat of summer.

All: I acknowledged my sin to You, and I did not cover my iniquity; I said, "I will confess my transgressions to the LORD," and You forgave the iniquity of my sin.

God Forgives Us

Many times in the Bible, we see that God is a forgiving God. What proof of God's forgiving nature do you find in these passages?

a. 2 Samuel 12:7–9, 13

b. 2 Chronicles 7:11–15

c. Mark 2:1–12

d. Luke 23:32–34

e. John 8:2–11

Because Jesus suffered and died in our place, God has forgiven, and continues to forgive, all our sins. Jesus tells us in the Lord's Prayer to ask for forgiveness. Because we know God's love, we can believe we are forgiven. We can go again and again to God for mercy.

We Forgive Others

We have learned from 1 John 4 that we love God and others because He first loved us. The same is true of forgiveness. A Christian's willingness to forgive others flows from gratitude and appreciation of God's love and forgiveness. Christians practice "bearing with one another and, if one has a complaint against another, forgiving each other; as the Lord has forgiven you, so you also must forgive" (Colossians 3:13).

1. Suppose you have a fight with a classmate. During the fight, he or she says some very nasty things to you. You are very upset about the fight. You want to forgive the classmate, but you just can't get that bitterness out of your heart, no matter how hard you try. So you ask God to forgive you. Will He? If so, why? If not, why not?

2. Change now from a "suppose" situation to a real situation. Think about a time you hurt a friend by what you said or did, or a friend hurt you. How did you feel? What did you do later to rebuild the friendship? Is there something you can do right now? To begin, spend some time in silent prayer. Ask God to forgive you. Also ask Him to lead you to do the right thing. Then plan some things you will do with this friend today and tomorrow.

To Review and Remember

Be kind to one another, tenderhearted, forgiving one another, as God in Christ God forgave you. *Ephesians 4:32*

The Fifth Petition and its explanation

The Sixth Petition—God's Protection

We Turn to God's Word

Temptations to sin abound. Everywhere we turn, we have opportunity and excuses to give in. Resisting sin is hard. And in our lives, sin often wins.

1. Read about sin's victory in Genesis 3:1–6.
a. Who was tempted?

b. What was the temptation?

c. Was the temptation to sin resisted successfully?

2. Read about sin's defeat in Matthew 4:1–11.
a. Who was tempted?

b. What was the temptation?

c. Was the temptation to sin resisted successfully?

nature—try to lure us away from God, tempting us to ignore or abandon God's will and promises. We ask in this petition that God would watch over us and keep us so that we are ready and able at all times to say no when these enemies confront us.

In your own words, tell what Scripture suggests for our confrontations with temptations.

a. James 4:7

Adam faced Satan and gave in to temptation. Jesus, the second Adam, faced Satan and resisted and won. Adam brought sin and death to all. Christ, the second Adam, through His obedience and death, brought righteousness and life to all. Jesus showed that with His help we, too, can overcome temptation.

Tempted by Evil

Read the Sixth Petition and its meaning. As in the Third Petition, three great enemies who seek to prevent God's will from taking place are identified. These evil forces—the devil, the world, and our sinful

b. Romans 12:2

c. Romans 13:14

3. Matthew 15:21–28

God uses the struggles and perplexities of this life to make us stronger. See James 1:2–3; Romans 5:1–5; 1 Peter 1:6–7. What are some of the ways God tests our faith today?

Tested by God

Luther states strongly and clearly that God does not tempt us. He bases his convictions on Bible passages such as James 1:13. But God indeed tests us, just as He tested His people throughout biblical history. God uses the testing of our faith to bring us closer to Him. Look at the following passages and explain how God tested the person mentioned in the text.

1. Genesis 22:1–19

The Sixth Petition

And lead us not into temptation.

What does this mean?

God tempts no one. We pray in this petition that God would guard and keep us so that the devil, the world, and our sinful nature may not deceive us or mislead us into false belief, despair, and other great shame and vice. Although we are attacked by these things, we pray that we may finally overcome them and win the victory.

2. John 6:1–14

To Review and Remember

Watch and pray that you may not enter into temptation. *Mark 14:38*

Be sober-minded; be watchful. Your adversary the devil prowls around like a roaring lion, seeking someone to devour. Resist him, firm in your faith. *1 Peter 5:8–9*

Put on the whole armor of God, that you may be able to stand against the schemes of the devil. *Ephesians 6:11*

The Sixth Petition and its explanation

39 The Seventh Petition and the Conclusion— God's Deliverance

The Seventh Petition

But deliver us from evil.

What does this mean?

We pray in this petition, in summary, that our Father in heaven would rescue us from every evil of body and soul, possessions and reputation, and finally, when our last hour comes, give us a blessed end, and graciously take us from this valley of sorrow to Himself in heaven.

The Conclusion

For Thine is the kingdom and the power and the glory forever and ever. Amen.

What does this mean?

This means that I should be certain that these petitions are pleasing to our Father in heaven, and are heard by Him; for He Himself has commanded us to pray in this way and has promised to hear us. Amen, amen, which means "yes, yes, it shall be so."

Living within God's Protection

In John 17, Jesus prayed for His people who are in this world.

1. What protection and blessing did He pray for His disciples? See verses 11, 13, 15.

2. What purpose do His disciples have in the world?

3. In addition to the disciples present in the room at that time, for whom did Jesus pray?

4. What is Jesus' prayer for the ultimate care and protection of His people?

5. In your own words, what assurance did Jesus give His people? See John 16:33.

God Delivers Us from Evil in Life

In this petition, we ask God to protect and deliver us from all the evil that may touch our lives, as Luther notes: "poverty, shame, death, and, in short, all the agonizing misery and heartache of which there is such an unnumbered multitude on the earth" (Large Catechism, The Lord's Prayer 115).

1. Read Psalm 91. Sometimes, God keeps evil from coming to us, and sometimes, God removes the evils that have touched our lives. List examples from the Bible where God delivered someone. Include incidents from your own life where God helped you.

2. God does not always deliver us from evil so directly. Sometimes, He uses difficulties and disasters and turns them to good for us and others. He gives us faith and strength to bear the evils, even though they are caused by Satan and sin. The apostle Paul certainly had plenty of problems. Read 2 Corinthians 11:24–28; 12:7–10. Briefly tell of Paul's troubles.

In response to Paul's plea for help, God said, "My grace is sufficient for you" (12:9). God's great power was working even during Paul's weakest moments. What great things did God accomplish through the ministry of Paul?

In short, even though we may struggle in life, God is constantly delivering us from evil—from the consequences of our own sin and from the stinging attacks of the devil. As Luther said: "For unless God preserved us, we would not be safe from this enemy even for an hour" (Large Catechism, The Lord's Prayer 116).

God Delivers Us from Evil at Death

The ultimate evil is death. Death is the result of sin. Since we have sinned, we must die. But God uses even death to achieve His purposes. Death brings an end to all our temptations, sins, and troubles. Through death, we enter the world of perfection that John described in the Book of Revelation.

1. Read John's vision of heaven in Revelation 21:1–4; 22:1–5. Then write what you imagine or what you expect heaven to be like.

2. Prepare your own list of evils that will end when we die.

None of us knows exactly what heaven will be like, but you have probably described your idea of a perfect place. And you can be sure that heaven will be a place of perfection and joy as we live eternally with God! With God's assurance of a place in heaven, some Christians may long to leave this world or go into seclusion. God, however, does not see life as something to escape or to avoid. He says we have a job to do—to live as people of God, telling the message of His love and salvation and serving Him and others.

Concluding Remarks

As the Lord's Prayer comes to an end, we wish to praise God and show our confidence that He will indeed answer our prayer. Read Catechism Question 235. List and explain three reasons why we may approach God with confidence.

a. First, God can and will take care of us because He alone is the _____ who has all good gifts in His control.

b. Second, we are confident God will answer our prayers because He alone has the _____ to grant our petitions.

c. Third, as God answers the prayers of His people, He deserves all the glory and is _____ of our praise.

To Review and Remember

The Lord will rescue me from every evil deed and bring me safely into His heavenly kingdom. To Him be the glory forever and ever. Amen. *2 Timothy 4:18*

Call upon Me in the day of trouble; I will deliver you, and you shall glorify Me. *Psalm 50:15*

The Seventh Petition and its explanation

The Conclusion of the Lord's Prayer

40 The Nature of Baptism—Not Simple Water Only

What a Mess!

It started out as a little white lie. Chelsey told her friend that she had to do homework that night so she wouldn't be able to go to the concert with her. But she didn't really have homework. Chelsey had made other plans that she didn't want her friend to know about, so she told just one little lie.

But as often happens, one little lie leads to other little lies, which in turn lead to bigger lies until we find ourselves embroiled in a confusing relationship mess. Our friends are mad—even the ones whose feelings we were trying to spare.

Have you ever found yourself in a real mess like this, or even worse? This kind of mess cannot be cleaned up with a little water and soap; it is a mess that seemingly has no "fix." Life gets very messy when we interact with fellow sinners.

The Bible says that our lives are a mess. We are born sinful. Our sinful nature, the world around us, and the devil conspire to lead us into sin every day of our lives. We don't have to think very hard to remember the last time we sinned. Take a mental run-through of this checklist that reviews the Ten Commandments, noting where you have messed up.

☐ Put God first.
☐ Honor and praise God's name.
☐ Hear and follow His Word.
☐ Obey those in authority.
☐ Help, not hurt, others.
☐ Regard others with decency.
☐ Protect people's possessions.
☐ Speak well of others.
☐ Be content with what you have.
☐ Respect people's relationships.

It is difficult to get a stain out of a shirt or to clean up spilled paint or oil. It is even more difficult to "clean up" our sin. It takes more than just water. Our strongest personal effort is not enough. But God has provided a way!

What a Solution!

Over and over again in the New Testament, and especially in the Book of Acts, we see people who, by God's grace, recognized their sinful condition and the need to be made clean.

1. Read the passages that follow. What sins were being recognized?
a. Acts 2:36–38

b. Acts 16:23–33

c. Acts 22:3–16

2. What happened in each of these situations?

Baptism is a means provided by God for cleansing our lives of sin and providing the power of the Holy Spirit for a new life.

A Visible Element

The word *baptize* means "to wash" or to apply water to a person in some way—to sprinkle, pour, wash, or immerse. Scripture contains stories of many kinds of washing with water. Naaman washed in the Jordan River and was healed (2 Kings 5:1–14); Pharisees washed their hands in traditional ceremonies of purification (Mark 7:1–4); God "washed" the entire earth and saved Noah and his family (1 Peter 3:18–21). But these are not what we call the Sacrament of Baptism.

Read Matthew 28:19. What does Jesus command?

Read Mark 16:16. What does Jesus say about Baptism?

Note that just as God has given us the Ten Commandments and the Lord's Prayer, He Himself gives us the command to baptize. It is not a human invention but a divine gift, by which we receive grace and love from God.

Water is a necessary, visible element for Baptism. But the important thing in the Sacrament is not the water or the way the water is applied, but that it is applied along with the Word of God. Baptism is more than simply washing with water. In Luther's words, Christian Baptism requires both God's command and God's Word, in addition to the visible, outward element of water.

Combined with the Word of God

In the Sacraments, a visible element—such as the water of Baptism—is joined to God's Word. Christ connected Baptism to His Word and to Himself with His instruction to baptize in the name of the Trinity: Father, Son, and Holy Spirit (see Matthew 28:19).

What is "the Word of God"? Write a brief summary.

Combined with the sure promise of salvation through Christ, the water of Baptism has the power to cleanse us from the stain of sin and empower us for new life in Christ.

The Nature of Baptism

What is Baptism?

Baptism is not just plain water, but it is the water included in God's command and combined with God's word.

Which is that word of God?

Christ our Lord says in the last chapter of Matthew: "Therefore go and make disciples of all nations, baptizing them in the name of the Father and of the Son and of the Holy Spirit." [Matthew 28:19]

To Review and Remember

Go therefore and make disciples of all nations, baptizing them in the name of the Father and of the Son and of the Holy Spirit. *Matthew 28:19*

The Nature of Baptism

41 The Nature of Baptism— God's Command and Promise

Mythbusting

As we will find when we discuss the lessons on the Lord's Supper, there are often myths we must "bust" in order to get to the heart of what these Sacraments truly are. What do they mean for us? Why are they important? What are some misconceptions about them? Let's look at some myths to try to accurately explain and understand Baptism. Read the Bible verses or catechism questions that come after each myth and rewrite each of these according to Scripture's clear teaching.

Myth 1. Baptism doesn't really do anything. It's just an outward symbol that doesn't have any lasting value. (Mark 16:16; 1 Peter 3:21)

Myth 2. Baptism isn't for everyone. Only people who understand its meaning should be baptized. (Matthew 28:19; Catechism Question 244)

Myth 3. The water used in Baptism itself has special powers.

Myth 4. A person who has never been baptized cannot be saved. (Mark 16:16)

Myth 5. Baptism automatically saves you, regardless whether you continue to believe in Jesus. (Mark 16:16)

Commissioned

Matthew 28:18–20 is called the Great Commission. A commission gives someone the authority (the right, duty, power) to do a special task for someone else. Read the Bible verses and answer the following questions.

1. Why did Jesus have the authority to give the Great Commission?

2. What three things did He command?

"Go therefore . . ."

3. What promise did Jesus give to accompany the Great Commission?

We, too, are disciples of Jesus: we have faith through the power of Baptism and God's Word. We, too, are commissioned: empowered by the Spirit to talk about our faith, knowing that Jesus is always with us.

Not everyone we speak to will immediately rush to church and be baptized. But God promises that His Word will accomplish its purpose, perhaps in ways we will never see.

Baptize All Nations

Christ's words "all nations" mean more than every country. They mean that He desires that every person—man, woman, and child—be baptized. Adults and older children (those old enough to learn) are taught about God before they are baptized. But what about babies and children too young to learn?

We baptize even the very youngest children for these reasons:

1. They are included in _____.
   (Matthew 28:19)

2. They are _____ and need God's forgiveness. (Psalm 51:5)

3. Through the _____ , children can _____ in God. (Acts 2:38–39; Matthew 18:6)

4. Jesus loves children and wants to _____ them. (Mark 10:16)

5. It can be expected that young children were included when the Early Church baptized entire _____. (Acts 16:15, 33)

6. Baptism and its blessings are not the result of what we do or what we know, for our faith in Christ is a_____ of God. (Ephesians 2:8)

By Baptism, even the youngest children become members of God's family and brothers and sisters of Jesus Himself. In addition, young children can experience God's forgiveness and love for them, and they can show their love for Jesus their Savior. In accordance with God's Word, we do not want to withhold the blessings of Baptism from them!

Continuing On . . .

Earlier in the lesson, we learned that Jesus wants us to spread His love and Word of salvation right where we are. But there was more to His message. As you read His message, add words to fit your situation. Jesus said, "You will be My witnesses in Jerusalem [your city: _____] and in all Judea [your country: _____] and Samaria [a neighboring country: _____], and to the end of the earth [several faraway countries: _____]" (Acts 1:8).

That's a big job, and we need to work together. We can work together as a church. In what ways does our church work to fulfill this commission locally, nationally, and worldwide?

Now think about yourself. What can you do now in your immediate environment or wherever you may go? What can you "tell" about Jesus and the Christian life without preaching a sermon or perhaps without even saying a word? Write some possibilities and turn them into plans.

To Review and Remember

Repent and be baptized every one of you in the name of Jesus Christ for the forgiveness of your sins, and you will receive the gift of the Holy Spirit. For the promise is for you and for your children and for all who are far off, everyone whom the Lord our God calls to Himself. *Acts 2:38–39*

42 The Blessings of Baptism— Forgiveness, Life, and Salvation

A New Beginning

Megan and Sarah stood in the corner of the gym, planning a party for Saturday night. "Come on, can't we think of anyone else to invite?" Sarah asked excitedly. "How about Jennifer? Doesn't she live somewhere near you?"

Megan's lips tightened. "Not her—she's a teacher's pet! You wouldn't like her. She's not very . . ."

Just then Jennifer came around the corner with a look on her face that showed she had overheard Megan's words.

Sarah broke the awkward silence. "Well, I guess I'd better get home. See you tomorrow."

"Bye, Sarah," Megan responded softly.

As Megan walked home, she kept remembering the things she had said about Jennifer and about being caught saying them.

"Well, it's true," Megan said to the sidewalk. "Jennifer is a teacher's pet." But suddenly Megan was flooded with memories from the years Megan and Jennifer had been best friends. Ever since kindergarten, they had been inseparable. "When did it stop?" Megan wondered. "Middle school," she recalled, "that's when. We started at this huge school, and all of a sudden Jennifer had tons of friends, and I had hardly any."

Megan realized that Jennifer wasn't the one who stopped the friendship; she had done it herself. They'd grown up together at church. Jesus loved them both. She decided then and there to do something about this situation.

The next day at school, Megan went out of her way to find Jennifer. "I've been thinking," she said, her head hung down, "about what you overheard yesterday. I have to . . ."

"You don't have to apologize," Jennifer interrupted.

"Yes, I do," Megan replied. "I was wrong in saying that stuff about you. I don't like myself when I do that, and I don't like not being your friend. I asked God to forgive me; would you forgive me too? Can we go back to being friends again? If you could come to my party Saturday, it would be just like old times."

The Blessings of Baptism

Most of us entered the family of God through Baptism when we were very young. We may wonder what relevance this act, performed on our behalf so long ago, has for our life today. But the blessings of Baptism are ongoing and as significant as the ability to continue to draw our very breath.

1. Consider what God's Word says about Baptism. Study Colossians 2:12–15. When Martin Luther faced the struggles and challenges of his life and work, he is said to have found comfort and confidence in reminding himself, "I am baptized!" By faith, all the blessings of Baptism encourage and empower each believer. In the left-hand column of the box, write Luther's summary of the blessings of Baptism. See Catechism Question 248.

2. When Megan thought about the love Jesus had for both Jennifer and herself, she also felt encouragement and a renewed sense of direction as a baptized child of God. Think about the challenges and struggles you face in your life right now. Use the box at the top of the next page to reflect on the meaning of each of the blessings God has given you through Baptism for your life today.

Baptism	"I am baptized!"
a. Works	a.
b. Rescues	b.
c. Gives	c.

Baptism—A Miraculous Event

Answer the following questions to review the Bible's teaching about Baptism—the divinely ordained act through which, by faith, we receive the blessings of our Savior's life, death, and resurrection.

1. Skeptics may accuse us Christians of teaching salvation by grace through faith on one hand while believing we can save others by bringing them to Baptism on the other. Explain. See Catechism Question 249.

2. Do unbelievers who have been baptized also possess the blessings of Baptism (Question 250)? Explain.

3. Can unbaptized persons be saved (Question 251)? Explain.

4. Why are Christians not to seek any baptism other than the sacramental Baptism (Question 252)?

The Blessings of Baptism

What benefits does Baptism give?

It works forgiveness of sins, rescues from death and the devil, and gives eternal salvation to all who believe this, as the words and promises of God declare.

Which are these words and promises of God?

Christ our Lord says in the last chapter of Mark: "Whoever believes and is baptized will be saved, but whoever does not believe will be condemned." [Mark 16:16]

To Review and Remember

For as many of you who were baptized into Christ have put on Christ. *Galatians 3:27*

He has delivered us from the domain of darkness and transferred us to the kingdom of His beloved Son, in whom we have redemption, the forgiveness of sins. *Colossians 1:13–14*

You were washed, you were sanctified, you were justified in the name of the Lord Jesus Christ and by the Spirit of our God. *1 Corinthians 6:11*

The Blessings of Baptism

43 The Power of Baptism—The Word of God

Not the Paper . . .

Jeremy stood there looking at two pieces of paper. His two best friends had each paid what they owed him with a piece of paper. Jeremy sighed as he looked at the paper that said "IOU." He crumpled it up and threw it away. He looked at the other piece of paper, a $20 bill, and put it in his pocket.

Both were pieces of paper. What made the difference? If you look closely at a piece of U.S. paper money, you will see these words: "This note is legal tender for all debts, public and private." Those words and the promise of the government behind it provide the power that makes the difference.

Not the Water . . .

In Baptism, it is not the water that has the power, but the Word of God connected with the water. It is God's promise to forgive us and make us His own children through Christ Jesus. This Word provides the power! This makes the difference!

It's the Word of God

Let's take a closer look at this powerful Word. Let's look at the written Word and the Word made flesh.

1. God inspired some of His servants to write the Holy Bible, His written Word. The Holy Spirit works through this Word, and the Word in the Sacraments, to bring us to faith, to keep us in faith, and to empower us to live in faith. What does each Bible verse say about this Word?
a. John 20:31

b. 2 Timothy 3:16–17

c. Ephesians 6:17

d. Romans 15:4

2. Read John 1:1–14. As you read these words, remember that Jesus Himself is the Word of God made flesh. God's power and promise and plan are fulfilled in Jesus.

In Baptism, by faith, we receive Jesus in our hearts and lives: "In Christ Jesus you are all sons of God, through faith. For as many of you as were baptized into Christ have put on Christ. There is neither Jew nor Greek, there is neither slave nor free, there is no male and female, for you are all one in Christ Jesus. And if you are Christ's, then you are Abraham's offspring, heirs according to promise" (Galatians 3:26–29).

How can water do such great things?

Certainly not just water, but the word of God in and with the water does these things, along with the faith which trusts this word of God in the water. For without God's word the water is plain water and no Baptism. But with the word of God it is a Baptism, that is, a life-giving water, rich in grace, and a washing of the new birth in the Holy Spirit, as St. Paul says in Titus chapter three:

"He saved us through the washing of rebirth and renewal by the Holy Spirit, whom He poured out on us generously through Jesus Christ our Savior, so that, having been justified by His grace, we might become heirs having the hope of eternal life. This is a trustworthy saying." [Titus 3:5–8]

And Faith

If the Word of God gives the power to the water in Baptism, why does Luther add "along with the faith which trusts this word of God"? Think back again to the story of Jeremy. Why did he throw away the IOU? He didn't trust that friend's word; he rejected it.

Receive it or reject it? People do not receive the blessings of Baptism if they refuse to believe. The power of God is certainly present in Baptism, but people may reject it. The power of Baptism comes from the Word of God, and we take hold of this power by faith.

Here are several important things we know about faith:

- Faith is a gift of God, not something we create inside ourselves.
- Faith may come before Baptism (when someone hears the Word of God).
- Faith may come as a result of Baptism (as with infants).
- Faith is necessary for our salvation, but it is not necessary to give power to Baptism—God has already done that.
- Faith receives and accepts the blessings that come in Baptism: in other words, God's gift of faith enables us to receive God's gift of Baptism!

Back to the Value of Money

In the opening of the lesson, we learned that the value of money isn't worth much without the understanding that it is valuable. It's similar with Baptism, but there are also some big differences. Answer these questions to show these contrasts.

1. The $20 bill depends on human government for its value. Upon what does Baptism depend for its value?

2. The $20 bill's temporary value is insignificant. Describe the value of Baptism.

3. The value of a $20 bill changes. How is this different from Baptism?

To Review and Remember

Christ loved the church and gave Himself up for her, that He might sanctify her, having cleansed her by the washing of water with the word. *Ephesians 5:25b–26*

The Power of Baptism

91

44 Drowned, Yet Alive—I'm a New Person

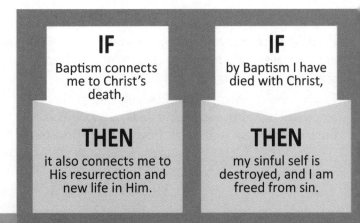

What Baptism Indicates

What does such baptizing with water indicate?

It indicates that the Old Adam in us should by daily contrition and repentance be drowned and die with all sins and evil desires, and that a new man should daily emerge and arise to live before God in righteousness and purity forever.

Where is this written?

St. Paul writes in Romans chapter six: "We were therefore buried with Him through baptism into death in order that, just as Christ was raised from the dead through the glory of the Father, we too may live a new life." [Romans 6:4]

The Old and the New

Whether or not we are baptized, we all have a sinful nature—a tendency or inclination to sin. Sometimes, this is called the "Old Adam." The sinful nature is a problem we face every day. How is this "Old Adam" in us drowned? See Catechism Question 256.

As the sinful nature in us is drowned daily as we repent and believe in God, the "new man" appears. What is our "new self" in Christ like? See Catechism Question 258.

Sin is a daily part of our lives, as is forgiveness. And we can be certain that our Baptism is also a daily part of our lives. Your Baptism is not just ancient history. It is not just your beginning as a Christian. It is a part of who you are now! What does it mean to you to be (or to become) a *baptized Christian?*

A life of repentance involves trust that God will forgive our sins. It involves a change in our heart, attitude, and life. Think of one specific attitude or action that you feel needs changing in your heart and life. Write a prayer to God for His help and strength to make a difference in you.

Dead and Alive

A piece of surprising news—and good news—is that, in a spiritual way, you and I are like the man who was "dead" and alive. Read Romans 6:3–11, and then study the diagram below to follow the apostle Paul's logic.

Through Christ, your sinful self is dead! Consider what differences and changes there will be as you live as a new person in Christ. What is new life in Christ like?

The New Life Begins

Use the Bible verses to help you answer the questions that follow.

1. How does God offer new life to us? What one thing is needed? See 1 Peter 1:23.

IF	IF
Baptism connects me to Christ's death,	by Baptism I have died with Christ,
THEN	**THEN**
it also connects me to His resurrection and new life in Him.	my sinful self is destroyed, and I am freed from sin.

2. Why baptize if only the Word is required? See Ephesians 5:25b–26.

3. In your own words, explain why "born again" is an appropriate synonym for Baptism. See Titus 3:5b–7.

4. In repentance, we daily receive the renewal of the blessings of Baptism—forgiveness and eternal life. As a class, answer the questions you or your sponsors may have answered or will answer at your Baptism:
Do you renounce the devil? Do you renounce all his works? Do you renounce all his ways?
Do you believe in God, the Father, . . . Son, . . . [and] Holy Spirit?
If you answer yes to these questions, you can be assured that, every day of your journey through life, God will provide the means for turning aside the power of Satan, for drowning the Old Adam in you, and for helping you to live as a new person in Christ.

Life, Led by the Spirit

Complete the following statements, showing how you, through Christ, willfully determine to live.

1. While my old self would like to laugh at someone's mistake, the new person in me

2. While my old self might think drinking or taking drugs will make me popular with others, the new person in me

3. While my old self wants to disobey when my parents tell me what to do, the new person in me

SINCE
I know Christ rose from death,

THEN
I know death no longer has power over me.

SINCE
the death He died was for all, and the life He lives is to God,

THEN
I can consider myself dead to sin and alive to God.

To Review and Remember

If anyone is in Christ, he is a new creation. *2 Corinthians 5:17*

Put on the new self, created after the likeness of God in true righteousness and holiness. *Ephesians 4:24*

For as many of you were baptized into Christ have put on Christ. *Galatians 3:27*

Put on then, as God's chosen ones, holy and beloved, compassionate hearts, kindness, humility, meekness, and patience, bearing with one another and, if one has a complaint against another, forgiving each other. . . . And above all these put on love. *Colossians 3:12–14*

What Baptism Indicates

45 Confession and Absolution— We Confess Our Sins to Our Waiting Father

Forgiveness Spoken

Jesus wanted everyone to receive the forgiveness He earned through His life and death. But there are those with hardened hearts toward God. They think they have no need of God, nor do they want anything to do with God's Church or His family. However, we are all in need of God's forgiveness and mercy, because we all fall under the burden of sin.

Read the Catechism section "What Is Confession?" (printed on the next page). Following the confession of our sins, God desires that we receive the comforting assurance of forgiveness. The spoken forgiveness is called *absolution.*

1. Look up the word *absolution.* What does it mean?

2. Who speaks the Absolution? See *Lutheran Service Book,* pages 290–93.

3. Why does the pastor speak this word of forgiveness to us?

Confessing Our Sins

Continue reading the sections on Confession from Martin Luther's Small Catechism (printed with this session).

1. Why do you think we should confess even "those [sins] we are not aware of"?

2. Dr. Luther suggests that you examine your everyday life, that you "consider your place in life according to the Ten Commandments" in order to recognize and confess your daily sinfulness. In the space below, list one of the commandments and explain how confession and forgiveness can help us live more as a son or daughter in God's family.

3. Read 1 John 1:9. How does the passage assure us that God forgives repentant sinners? Write the promise here:

It Sounds So Easy

Is that all there is to it? Just say, "I'm sorry, God," and through the pastor, He says "That's okay"? No! Confession and Absolution are more than that. Confession includes repentance—that sharp look inside ourselves at what is wrong and the sadness we feel at that sin. And then it involves telling, but not just God—who else? Try this example. You hurt someone by calling him a bad name in front of your friends.

1. In addition to going to God and saying, "I'm sorry, God—forgive me," what else needs to be done?

2. Why is this second step so difficult?

3. Sometimes, we may do something we feel is really bad—something that hurts or keeps on bothering us long after it is over. It bugs us, nags at us, makes us feel down. And even after we go to church and say the words about being sorry and hear the Absolution—we still feel bad about it. What then? Read the Catechism portion "What sins should we confess?" (at right). Where are we to go with sins that bother us? Why?

4. How do we know that the pastor will keep to himself that which we have confessed to him? See Catechism Question 267.

There are two different ways we can confess our sins—either corporately (with a group) or individually (by ourselves with the pastor). With either form, we can confess our sins and be assured of God's forgiveness. Thanks be to God!

What is confession?

Confession has two parts. First that we confess our sins, and second, that we receive absolution, that is, forgiveness, from the pastor as from God Himself, not doubting, but firmly believing that by it our sins are forgiven before God in heaven.

What sins should we confess?

Before God we should plead guilty of all sins, even those we are not aware of, as we do in the Lord's Prayer; but before the pastor we should confess only those sins which we know and feel in our hearts.

Which are these?

Consider your place in life according to the Ten Commandments: Are you a father, mother, son, daughter, husband, wife, or worker? Have you been disobedient, unfaithful, or lazy? Have you been hop-tempered, rude, or quarrelsome? Have you hurt someone by your words or deeds? Have you stolen, been negligent, wasted anything, or done any harm?

To Review and Remember

Whoever conceals his transgressions will not prosper, but he who confesses and forsakes them will obtain mercy. *Proverbs 28:13*

But if we walk in the light, as He is in the light, we have fellowship with one another, and the blood of Jesus His Son cleanses us from all sin. If we say we have no sin, we deceive ourselves, and the truth is not in us. If we confess our sins, He is faithful and just to forgive us our sins and to cleanse us from all unrighteousness. *1 John 1:7–9*

What is confession?

46 The Office of the Keys— Extending God's Forgiveness

1. Read Matthew 16:16–19. What does Peter confess about Jesus?

2. Upon this confession, what will Jesus build?

3. And what does Jesus give to Peter and the church?

4. What power does the church have with the keys of the kingdom of heaven?

5. Read Catechism Question 270. Explain the authority of the Office of the Keys.

6. Name at least four ways that the church proclaims forgiveness (see Catechism Question 271).

The Kingdom of God

During Jesus' earthly ministry, He often taught about the kingdom of heaven. He told parables to explain the Kingdom, such as the parable of the prodigal son, in which the father welcomes his son back home, even after the son squandered his father's money. Jesus also told about the lost coin and the lost sheep, whose owners search and search for their lost ones. Read about these three parables and fill in the chart on the following page.

What Is the Office of the Keys?

We know that heaven is a free gift in Jesus Christ. But how do people get into the Kingdom? Who can open the door for them?

Jesus gave the Office of the Keys and the power to extend or withhold forgiveness to the church, but the pastor has the role of exercising this authority. As the representative of Christ in the church (like the apostles), the pastor speaks Christ's forgiveness to repentant sinners and withholds forgiveness from the unrepentant (John 20:22–23).

Think of the example of a public park. A park can be a wonderful place to exercise, play sports, or just enjoy nature. A question to consider is this: to whom does the park belong? The park belongs to all of the people—to everyone in the community. But who is in charge of making changes or decisions regarding the park? Who holds the "keys" to the park? Usually this authority belongs to a person or a group of people.

Similarly, in the church, we appoint pastors as Christ's representatives to extend to us the grace and mercy of Christ through preaching, through Baptism, and through the Lord's Supper. We may be as certain in his proclamation of Christ's forgiveness as if Jesus Himself were speaking it to us.

What is the Office of the Keys?

The Office of the Keys is that special authority which Christ has given to His church on earth to forgive the sins of repentant sinners, but to withhold forgiveness from the unrepentant as long as they do not repent.

Where is this written?

This is what St. John the Evangelist writes in chapter twenty: The Lord Jesus breathed on His disciples and said, "Receive the Holy Spirit. If you forgive anyone his sins, they are forgiven; if you do not forgive them, they are not forgiven." [John 20:22–23]

Bible Verses	Who is lost?	What does the owner/guardian do?	How is this like the kingdom of heaven?
Luke 15:1–7	**A sheep**	**The shepherd leaves the remaining ninety-nine sheep to search for the lost one.**	**Verse 7—"There will be more joy in heaven over one sinner who repents . . ."**
Luke 15:8–10	**A coin**	**The woman lights a lamp and sweeps the house in order to find the coin.**	**Verse 10—"There is joy before the angels of God over one sinner who repents . . ."**
Luke 15:11–32	**A son**	**The father gives his inheritance to his ungrateful son, but then welcomes him home when all the money is squandered away.**	**Just as the father welcomes his son home, so also our heavenly Father welcomes sinners into the kingdom of heaven.**

To Review and Remember

You are a chosen race, a royal priesthood, a holy nation, a people for His own possession, that you may proclaim the excellencies of Him who called you out of darkness into His marvelous light. *1 Peter 2:9*

What is the Office of the Keys?

47 A Repentant Life—Forgiven and Forgiving

God's Great Love and Forgiveness

The story of Zacchaeus the tax collector can teach us a great deal about forgiveness.

1. Read Luke 19:1–2. How is Zacchaeus described?

2. Read Luke 19:3–4. Why did Zacchaeus climb the tree?

3. Read Luke 19:5. What did Jesus ask Zacchaeus to do? Did Zacchaeus do it?

4. Read Luke 19:6–8. What was Zacchaeus's response to Jesus' presence?

5. Read Luke 19:9. What blessings did Jesus say would come to Zacchaeus?

As He says in summary to Zacchaeus's story, Jesus came to "seek and to save the lost" (Luke 19:10). Zacchaeus, as a tax collector, would have been known as a public sinner. The tax collectors at that time were known to often take more money for the tax than was necessary in order to themselves become wealthy. As such, they were often despised due to their greed and wealth. So, for this "sinner," not a favorite of the crowds, to receive such an honor

from Jesus would have left the people grumbling. But that is exactly what Jesus came to do: He came to seek and to save the lost—the sinners, the outcast, and the sick.

1. What if Zacchaeus had said, "No thanks, Jesus. I don't want to come down. I'm just here to watch the parade"? Or what if he had run away from Jesus' invitation? Write some reasons why Zacchaeus (and we) might not accept the invitation to come down from our "sycamore trees." What excuses might we give for preferring to stay where we are?

2. Other things can prevent us from accepting God's forgiveness. A person may feel guilt over a past action, anguish over the hopelessness of a sinful human condition, or even doubt about the extent of God's forgiveness. Sometimes, we feel unnecessary guilt over things that shouldn't bother us, or we know we've been forgiven by God but can't seem to forgive ourselves. Read Isaiah 1:18. Write the assuring words of God's complete and unconditional forgiveness here:

Excuses or Confession?

How would you respond to the following situations? Do these people seem like they are truly sorry for their sins?

1. "The teacher shouldn't have made the test so hard. Yeah, I cheated, but big deal. Everyone did."
2. "I was at the convenience store with my friend and didn't have enough money to pay for the snack I wanted. I just stuck the package in my coat. I can't stop thinking about how wrong it was, though."
3. "I downloaded some songs online from a pirated Web site. Who cares? Those rock stars are rich anyway."
4. "I know I shouldn't have lied to Amanda when she asked if I'd been at the party. I feel terrible."

1. Dealing with people who have sinned and come to us for help. (See Philemon 15–16.)

2. "Making right" wrongs that are in the past. (See Philemon 18–19.)

3. Who should be involved in the forgiveness process. (See Philemon 8–9.)

Responding to Forgiveness

Zacchaeus didn't wait long to show that he received God's saving love. He acted like a new person immediately. The Zacchaeus who shared his treasure was not the same one Jesus called down from the sycamore tree.

Similarly, Paul, who went to Damascus blind, was not the same man who had persecuted Christians. Paul became one of God's great missionaries. He was a leader among the churches and traveled across the known world spreading the Gospel. During his life, many troubles came to Paul—most of them as a result of his witness for Jesus. Finally, he ended up in prison.

While Paul was in prison, an escaped slave named Onesimus (O-NESS-ee-mus) came to him. Onesimus had run away from his master, Philemon (Fah-LEE-mon), who was a friend of Paul, and sought out Paul for help and safety. Onesimus stayed with Paul for a time and served him. In order to make the situation right—especially since Onesimus may have taken property from his master—Paul wrote a letter. The letter, called Philemon, is in our Bible. Write what we can learn from Paul's example about the following:

To Review and Remember

Though your sins are like scarlet, they shall be as white as snow; though they are red like crimson, they shall become like wool. *Isaiah 1:18*

The sacrifices of God are a broken spirit; a broken and contrite heart, O God, You will not despise. *Psalm 51:17*

I acknowledged my sin to You, and did not cover up my iniquity; I said, "I will confess my transgressions to the LORD," and You forgave the iniquity of my sin. *Psalm 32:5*

Let all bitterness and wrath and anger and clamor and slander be put away from you, along with all malice. Be kind to one another, tenderhearted, forgiving one another, as God in Christ forgave you. *Ephesians 4:31–32*

48 Pastor and People—Shepherd and Sheep

Our Shepherd, Jesus

Who is the pastor of your church? The true Shepherd, or Pastor of the Church, is Jesus. He is the One who forgives sins, loves His Bride, the Church, and gathers us together as one in Him.

1. Read John 10:1–11. How does Jesus describe the relationships of a shepherd and his sheep?

2. In these verses, how does Jesus describe Himself?

Sometimes, sheep get a bad reputation as being gullible or not too smart. But the truth is that sheep, according to these verses, actually can distinguish between the voice of a stranger and the voice of their shepherd. That shows at least some level of discernment. Maybe they are a little like our pets, our dogs in particular. They recognize their master, know their favorite person's voice, and respond better to that person than to anyone else.

The shepherd here is shown as a selfless leader who would even go so far as to lay down his life for his sheep, if the need arose. The shepherd is portrayed as one who would forsake his own needs and wants in order to care for and help his sheep. This perfectly describes our Shepherd, Jesus, who gave everything, even His own life to care for us and forgive our sins.

Our Pastor, or "Undershepherd"

The image of shepherd and sheep is how we should think about the role of the pastor and people in the church. We begin with the understanding that Jesus is our true Shepherd, the One who has laid down His life for His sheep—for all who belong to His Holy Church. Then, we further understand that our individual pastors in congregations are like "undershepherds." They act in Christ's stead, or "stand in" for Jesus. When on Sunday morning, our

pastor announces Christ's forgiveness, it is as though Christ Himself is forgiving us. When the pastor shares God's Word with us, it is as though Christ Himself is speaking to us. When the pastor serves us at the Lord's Supper, it is as though Christ Himself is giving His very body and blood to us. He is separate from the congregation in that he is the representative of Christ's love and forgiveness; however, undershepherds are also sheep in Christ's Church as well, along with all Christians.

How Are Pastors Chosen?

Jesus Himself selected His twelve disciples, or apostles, to be the first servants of His church. These twelve men, along with others, including the apostle Paul, carried on the work of sharing the good news of salvation with others and proclaiming God's Word. Who were some of these first pastors of the faith? Read the following verses to find out and match the verses with the answers shown:

Acts 2:14 ○	○ Timothy
Acts 8:5, 12 ○	○ Peter
Acts 14: 9–10 ○	○ Paul
1 Timothy 1:2; 3:1–5 ○	○ Philip
Acts 15:12 ○	○ Paul and Barnabas

Today, pastors are chosen in order to represent Christ within the church and to act as "undershepherds" for the sheep, or Christians, in local congregations. We choose our pastors in a similar way to the manner in which the Early Church chose their leaders.

First, we follow the guidelines of Scripture. Read the following verses and describe who should be a pastor:

a. 1 Timothy 3:1–2

b. 2 Timothy 2:2; 15

We also follow the model of Scripture in allowing men to lead our congregation in the place of our Savior, Jesus. Once we have met, to the best of our ability, the guidelines of Scripture, we use our God-given reason and faith in order to come together as a congregation and choose that pastor we think could lead in our particular situation. We choose that pastor who would best lead us. So, in summary, who should be considered for the office of the pastor? See Catechism Question 278.

Clearly, such a comparison teaches that all parts of the body are different and all parts are necessary. We all have gifts, and we all have the command to use them as Christ's representatives on earth.

Even though the pastor is the spiritual leader in the congregation, he is not able to do all of the work necessary to support a congregation. Everyone in the church must help.

1. Who are his helpers? How do they help?

2. Read 1 Corinthians 12:12–27. What is St. Paul telling us about our place in the Church?

Our Mission in Christ

Christ gave all His disciples a command to go into all the world and tell His Good News to everybody. The command is for every disciple. He gives each member the gifts necessary to carry out His command. Read Ephesians 4:7, 11–16.

1. According to verse 7, who receives God's gift?

2. Verse 11 lists some of the gifts of Christ. The positions listed are different, but all are given for the same purposes. What are the purposes?

3. Verses 15–16 compare the relationship between Christ and those who serve Him to the head of the body and the parts of that body. In order for this "body" to grow in love, what kind of relationship is necessary in the body?

What do you believe according to these words?

I believe that when the called ministers of Christ deal with us by His divine command, in particular when they exclude openly unrepentant sinners from the Christian congregation and absolve those who repent of their sins and want to do better, this is just as valid and certain, even in heaven, as if Christ our dear Lord dealt with us Himself.

To Review and Remember

Just as the body is one and has many members, and all the members of the body, though many, are one body, so it is with Christ. *1 Corinthians 12:12*

If anyone aspires to the office of overseer [pastor], he desires a noble task. Therefore an overseer must be above reproach, the husband of one wife, sober-minded, self-controlled, respectable, hospitable, able to teach. *1 Timothy 3:1–2*

Do your best to present yourself to God as one approved, a worker who has no need to be ashamed, rightly handling the word of truth. *2 Timothy 2:15*

49 Church Discipline and Excommunication— Difficult Decisions

We Live in a Broken World

One of the favorite phrases used in children's stories is "and they lived happily ever after." When we are young, we believe in a world like that. Wouldn't it be wonderful if it were true—if everyone were honest and kind, if quarrels never happened, and if bad days went away like bad dreams in the morning?

But we're old enough now to know better. We already know that people often fail, and real life is not always lived happily ever after. One thing we learn even as children is that the same people who help and love us can often hurt us. Think about times like that. How did you feel? What would you have liked to do to the person who hurt you? How does it feel to remember it now?

When Others Sin against Us

Jesus gives us some suggestions for dealing with imperfect people and broken relationships in Matthew 18:15–18. Read the passage.

1. List the three steps for dealing with someone who has sinned.

   a.

   b.

   c.

2. The last part of verse 15 mentions the reason these steps should be taken; the reason is not to get rid of the person or to hurt him. Write the reason below.

When sin has broken a relationship, the hope is always restoration. We always want to restore peace and love to a difficult situation. "Gained your brother," as described in Matthew 18, is to try to bring peace to that broken relationship, to encourage repentance and humility so that we, as imperfect sinners, can live in peace and harmony.

Church Discipline

The process outlined in the previous section is called "church discipline." Its purpose is to give those living in open sin every chance to see what they are doing, to repent, and to return to God and His church. Living in "open sin" means that the person is either not aware of or not sorry for a sin he or she is committing. These steps, when undertaken by a congregation, are done slowly. It is not enough simply to take each step and hurry on to the next in order to get the process over with. Since the purpose of the action is to save the sinner, each step—the individual confrontation, the small group, and the congregational effort—should be tried several times before we assume we have failed.

1. Read Matthew 18:21–22. What question is Peter asking Jesus?

2. What conclusion can be drawn from Jesus' answer?

Excommunication

Sometimes, even repeated efforts fail to help a sinner repent. The church, through the Office of the Keys, has the power—and the responsibility—to take an action to separate the unrepentant sinner from the congregation. This action is called "excommunication." Excommunication is a serious step and must be done with great care.

Choose the correct reason(s) for excommunication from this list. Be prepared to defend your choice on the basis of Scripture.

_____ 1. To get rid of a bad sinner

_____ 2. To show the world that sinners are not welcome in church

_____ 3. To help a person realize his or her sinfulness and repent

_____ 4. To keep the church pure

_____ 5. To keep certain people away from other believers

The saddest and most difficult part of the Office of the Keys is the pastor's duty to announce that the congregation has excommunicated a member. It is a time for prayer on the part of pastor and congregation that the excommunicated person would repent and return to God.

The Return of the Sinner

1. Of what does the apostle Paul remind us in Romans 3:23?

2. Look at Matthew 18:15–18 again. Now look at the verses just before that section (vv. 10–14). There, Jesus tells about the man who had one hundred sheep and left the ninety-nine to search for the one that was lost. Read verse 14 and write Jesus' words of hope below.

3. The love that searches for the lost one is the model the Christian congregation must follow. If at any time the excommunicated person comes back, repents, and asks for reinstatement in the congregation, the answer is always yes. The door is always open. The congregation, like Christ Himself, encourages and invites such a return. The congregation, like Christ, must "have no pleasure in the death of anyone," but desires that all should "turn, and live" (Ezekiel 18:32).

How does Jesus' parable of the lost son (Luke 15:11–32) teach this truth?

To Review and Remember

Brothers, if anyone is caught in any transgression, you who are spiritual should restore him in a spirit of gentleness. Keep watch of yourself, lest you too be tempted. Bear one another's burdens, and so fulfill the law of Christ. *Galatians 6:1–2*

Peter came up and said to [Jesus], "Lord, how often will my brother sin against me, and I forgive him? As many as seven times?" Jesus said to him, "I do not say to you seven times, but seventy-seven times." *Matthew 18:21–22*

50 The Nature of the Sacrament of the Altar— A Gift from the Lord

A Sacrament

Passion Week began with Palm Sunday, when Jesus rode triumphantly into Jerusalem, and ended with Easter, when Jesus rose from the dead. One of the events during that week was the institution of the Lord's Supper. On Thursday, Jesus gathered with His disciples in the Upper Room for one last meal together. This was the night before Jesus would be crucified. It was during this meal that Jesus established the Lord's Supper as His gift of forgiveness and grace to His followers.

What do we call something that

a. is instituted by God;

b. uses visible elements that are joined to God's Word; and

c. offers, gives, and assures believers of the forgiveness of sins through Christ?

A_____

There are two of these:

1. Baptism—which we may receive

O_____

2. The Lord's Supper—which we may receive

O_____

Note: Sometimes, Holy Absolution is counted as a third sacrament, even though it has no divinely instituted visible element (Large Catechism: Baptism 74 and The Apology of the Augsburg Confession, Article XIII 4).

The Gift of Forgiveness

Jesus gave this meal to strengthen our faith, forgive our sins, and draw us closer to Him. When we receive the body and blood of Jesus Himself, we are being strengthened spiritually—and we all need more faith. As the father of the sick girl in Mark 9:24 stated to Jesus: "I believe; help my unbelief!" Because of the "old Adam" or sinful nature that tugs us toward sin every day, we need to be renewed in our faith daily as well. The Lord's Supper assures us of God's love and mercy toward us and strengthens our faith.

Sometimes, people might think: "Oh, I don't need Communion again. I just had it two weeks ago." But the truth is that we need more faith, more grace every day. We daily sin much and fall short. We disobey the Ten Commandments. We have sinful thoughts and behaviors. The truth is that we need the grace provided for us in the Sacrament of the Altar.

Read Catechism Questions 291 and 296. Then complete the following by writing your answers in the corresponding sections below.

Box 1: The Lord's Supper is not just bread and wine. Mere bread and wine have no spiritual power. What must be connected with the visible elements?

Boxes 2 and 3: The Lord's Supper is bread and wine and much, much more. As stated by Christ Himself, what do we receive in, with, and under the bread and wine?

Boxes A, B, C: What are some of the blessings we receive in this Sacrament?

In 1 Corinthians 11:26, we read that when you receive the Lord's Supper "you proclaim the Lord's death until He comes." In addition to receiving blessings, you are declaring your faith and giving glory to God because Jesus died on the cross for you. Outline the diagram in the shape of a cross and praise God for His great gifts to you!

Miracles, Miracles!

Think about another meal Jesus provided. Think about Jesus on a hillside with His disciples and over five thousand other people. Read Matthew 14:15–21 and 26:26–28.

1. What are some similarities between the two meals?

2. What are some of the differences?

3. Tell why the Lord's Supper is important to you. Why do you want to receive Holy Communion?

The Nature of the Sacrament of the Altar

What is the Sacrament of the Altar?

It is the true body and blood of our Lord Jesus Christ under the bread and wine, instituted by Christ Himself for us Christians to eat and to drink.

Where is this written?

The holy Evangelists Matthew, Mark, Luke, and St. Paul write: Our Lord Jesus Christ, on the night when He was betrayed, took bread, and when He had given thanks, He broke it and gave it to the disciples and said: "Take, eat; this is My body, which is given for you. This do in remembrance of Me."

In the same way also He took the cup after supper, and when He had given thanks, He gave it to them, saying, "Drink of it, all of you; this cup is the new testament, in My blood, which is shed for you for the forgiveness of sins. This do, as often as you drink it, in remembrance of Me."

	1		
2	bread	wine	3
	A		
	B		
	C		

To Review and Remember

They devoted themselves to the apostles' teaching and the fellowship, to the breaking of bread and the prayers. *Acts 2:42*

The Nature of the Sacrament of the Altar

The Sacrament of the Altar—"In Remembrance"

Mythbusting

The following statements about the Lord's Supper are myths, or falsehoods. Tell why you disagree with each statement as you consider what is the truth about the Lord's Supper. (Refer to the Bible verses and Catechism sections indicated.)

Myth 1. God's Word is not necessary in order to have the Lord's Supper (Question 291).

Myth 2. Only those who have avoided great sin or who are strong in faith should receive the Sacrament (Mark 9:24; John 6:37).

Myth 3. In the Sacrament of the Altar, the bread and wine are symbols, or no more than reminders to us of the body and blood of Christ (Question 287).

Myth 4. The same benefits of the Sacrament are offered to all who take Communion, regardless of their attitude or belief (1 Corinthians 11:27–29).

Myth 5. The bread and wine change into body and blood (transubstantiation) and are no longer bread and wine (1 Corinthians 10:16).

Myth 6. The Sacrament of the Altar is a resacrifice of Christ's body and blood (Hebrews 10:10, 14, 18).

Myth 7. Celebrating the Lord's Supper once a year, like any anniversary, is often enough (Acts 2:42).

Myth 8. It doesn't matter if we use actual bread and wine. Anything will do (Matthew 26:26–27).

The Truth

Check any statements that describe the Lord's Supper.

☐ 1. A Witness—In the Sacrament, you confess your faith in Christ.

☐ 2. A Eucharist—A time of thanksgiving, joy, and praise to God.

☐ 3. A Remembering—You are reminded of Christ's sacrifice for your sins.

☐ 4. A Communion—A time to unite, to be joined together with God and other believers.

☐ 5. A Banquet of Love—A celebration where God's love is showered on you. You, in turn, living in Christ, share love with others.

Actually, the Lord's Supper is not just one of the above, it is all of these. Most significantly, it is this:

☐ 6. A Gift of God—A blessing offering forgiveness, life, and salvation through Christ, our Savior, who died and arose for us. It is a blessing of eternal consequence!

"May the God of endurance and encouragement grant you to live in such harmony with one another, in accord with Christ Jesus, that together you may with one voice glorify the God and Father of our Lord Jesus Christ" (Romans 15:5–6).

To Review and Remember

As often as you eat this bread and drink the cup, you proclaim the Lord's death until He comes.
1 Corinthians 11:26

The Nature of the Sacrament of the Altar

52 The Benefit of the Sacrament of the Altar— Strengthening Your Faith

In Training

Karl, a sophomore at a state university, is sitting at the team training table eating whole-grain bread, lean meat, and plenty of vegetables. In the past, he had followed his natural inclination to spend all his time with friends at fast-food restaurants, filling up with burgers and shakes. The result was flab, fatigue, freshman failure, and no football.

However, Karl's coach changed all that. Now Karl follows a menu that is helping him grow stronger and healthier and an exercise plan that keeps him active. It isn't easy, but he has lots of support. He feels that he's part of the team.

Karl had a problem; his coach had a plan. Now let's look at a bigger problem we all have and at God's greater plan.

A Faith-Strengthening Meal

We are, by nature, sinful and prone to sin, but God changes that. He has a plan for us that is centered in forgiveness through Jesus' death and resurrection. He calls us to repentance, leading us to confess our sins and turn to new life in Christ. And He has a plan to help us continue in faith, growing stronger and healthier spiritually. Read Acts 2:42 and then list four ways that God strengthens our faith.

1.

2.

3.

4.

With Whom Do You Eat?

The apostle Paul was concerned about some Christians who were eating the meat sacrificed to idols. See 1 Corinthians 10:14–21. By association, they were becoming partners with unbelievers and participants in their worship.

Instead, in verses 16–17, Paul calls the Christians to eat the Lord's Supper with other faithful Christians, and by association, affirm that they believed the same Word and promise of God.

This section of Scripture clearly points out that when we take the Sacrament—or refuse to take it, for that matter—we are speaking a powerful message to others.

1. What does our participation say about our relationship to Christ?

2. What does it say to the others communing with us?

This is a significant witness declaring with whom we are united by faith in Christ.

The Benefits of the Sacrament

What are the benefits for your body when you eat healthy foods such as lean meat, fruit, and vegetables?

As stated in Matthew 26:28, the benefit of eating at the Lord's Table is forgiveness. But there are other benefits flowing from forgiveness. "For where there is forgiveness of sins, there is also life and salvation."

1. How are forgiveness, eternal life, and salvation related?

2. What benefits do hearing God's Word and eating at the Lord's Table have for a Christian's daily life?

What Is Forgiveness?

We toss around the word *forgiveness* so much that we tend to take it for granted and maybe even take it lightly. The Bible tells us that God humbled Himself, became one of us, and took the punishment for our sins.

1. Forgiveness is not easy—Christ paid a high cost for our forgiveness on the cross. Review the explanation of the Second Article of the Apostles' Creed and quote how Jesus paid the price for our forgiveness and why He did it:

2. When we understand the great forgiveness and mercy of God, when we understand that we belong to Him, we learn to forgive too. It is not easy. But we are not alone. God is with us. What does He use to strengthen, comfort, support, and encourage us?

The Benefit of the Sacrament of the Altar
What is the benefit of this eating and drinking?

These words, "Given and shed for you for the forgiveness of sins," show us that in the Sacrament forgiveness of sins, life, and salvation are given us through these words. For where there is forgiveness of sins, there is also life and salvation.

To Review and Remember
The Benefit of the Sacrament of the Altar

53 Power in the Sacrament—Given *for You*

Power in Action

1. Read Acts 2:1–13. Summarize the event. What is happening in these verses?

2. Verses 14–36 record the powerful sermon Peter preached to the people who had assembled.
a. What event is the focus of his sermon? See verses 22–24.

b. What was the result of Peter's preaching? See verses 37–41.

c. Peter used strong words. He spoke the Word of God (the Good News of salvation in Jesus Christ). What power made three thousand people repent and believe? See verse 33.

2. Who brings that power and puts it into effect, offering faith and forgiveness?

3. In your own words, finish these statements: Without the Word, the water in Baptism is

It cannot save us.

Without the Word, the bread and wine in Holy Communion is

The Power of the Sacraments

From the Catechism, read Baptism Part III: "The Power of Baptism" ("How can water do such great things?") and the Sacrament of the Altar Part III: "The Power of the Sacrament of the Altar" ("How can bodily eating and drinking do such great things?")

1. Where does the power of the Sacrament lie, according to both sections?

It cannot save us.

The visible elements of bread and wine are connected with God's Word to impart God's gracious gifts of forgiveness and grace. But is it truly necessary to use bread and wine in the Lord's Supper? Christ Himself used bread and wine, and there is no reason for us to differ from His institution.

III. The Power of the Sacrament of the Altar

How can bodily eating and drinking do such great things?

Certainly not just eating and drinking do these things, but the words written here: "Given and shed for you for the forgiveness of sins." These words, along with the bodily eating and drinking, are the main thing in the Sacrament. Whoever believes these words has exactly what they say: "forgiveness of sins."

God's grace and mercy to us is lavish! To each one who receives the Sacrament in faith, He gives us "the very same treasure that is appointed for me against my sins, death, and every disaster" (Large Catechism, Sacrament of the Altar 22).

4. Because of the strengthened faith we receive in the Lord's Supper, how often would God have us partake in this special meal?

Power for Us

Because the Holy Spirit is working through the Word, a powerful miracle happens in Communion. Instead of just bread and wine, Jesus also offers Himself to us.

1. What are the blessings we receive along with His body and blood?

2. How do we receive these blessings Christ offers in the Sacrament?

3. From the catechism, what is the most important part of the Sacrament of the Altar? Christ instituted the Sacrament, and it is "given and shed _____ _____ for the forgiveness of sins."

To Review and Remember

Trust in the LORD with all your heart, and do not lean on your own understanding. *Proverbs 3:5*

Blessed is she who believed that there would be a fulfillment of what was spoken to her from the Lord. *Luke 1:45*

Now faith is the assurance of things hoped for, the conviction of things not seen. *Hebrews 11:1*

The Power of the Sacrament of the Altar

54 How to Receive the Sacrament Worthily—Preparing for the Feast

The Church in Corinth

In the Early Church, Christians did not have church buildings, so believers usually gathered together in homes. Most likely, they met together in one of the wealthier member's homes. In 1 Corinthians 11:17–34, we learn a little bit about the church in Corinth, a city in Greece. In this very new congregation, the people were celebrating together on the Lord's Day (Sunday, the day of Jesus' resurrection; see Revelation 1:10) in a person's home. The group of people was likely large enough to spill over from one room to the next. Read about what was happening in these verses.

1. What was going wrong?

How to Receive This Sacrament Worthily
Who receives this sacrament worthily?

Fasting and bodily preparation are certainly fine outward training. But that person is truly worthy and well prepared who has faith in these words: "Given and shed for you for the forgiveness of sins."

But anyone who does not believe these words or doubts them is unworthy and unprepared, for the words "for you" require all hearts to believe.

2. How did Paul react to the misuse of the Lord's Supper?

Being Worthy

On our own merit, we are unworthy of the tremendous treasure that God gives in the Lord's Supper, and there is nothing we can do ourselves to make ourselves worthy before God. However, there is One who is worthy, and that is Jesus, the perfect Son of God. He lived a sinless life and then offered the perfect sacrifice for sins in His death on the cross. "For our sake [God] made Him to be sin who knew no sin, so that in Him we might become the righteousness of God" (2 Corinthians 5:21).

3. What do you think the people had forgotten?

4. What warning does Paul give to people who take the Sacrament unworthily?

With this in mind, read the Catechism section in the box above to answer this question: *What is the one thing needed for us to be worthy and prepared to receive the Lord's Supper?*

Being Unprepared

So, does it matter who receives the Sacrament? Does it matter how we receive the Sacrament? From the verses in 1 Corinthians 11, we learn that there were problems with the celebration of the Lord's Supper. There are also times when those who come to the altar are not fully prepared for the seriousness of the treasure God has given. Who, then, is unprepared and should not receive the Sacrament? See Catechism Question 305.

a.

b.

c.

d.

In order to help these people avoid the consequences of receiving the Lord's Supper to their judgment, our church practices "close" Communion, limiting the Sacrament to those who understand the Sacrament and are united in faith in Christ and in the words "given and shed for you for the forgiveness of sins."

Outward/Inward Preparations

Since Paul's time, Christians have been concerned about the best way to prepare for receiving the Sacrament. We respect the importance of this gift from God and want to be well prepared. So, what can we do to prepare ourselves?

Some churches practice individual confession and absolution, encouraging believers to repent, confess, and receive the individual proclamation of God's Word of forgiveness before receiving the Lord's Supper. Other churches practice corporate, or group, confession, in which all confess their sins together before receiving the Lord's body and blood.

Another excellent preparation for receiving the Lord's Supper is to review the Ten Commandments. Ask yourself the difficult questions: Have I disobeyed my authorities? Have I gossiped? Have I put God first in everything? These are the questions to review before approaching this gift from God.

1. Again, what is necessary for the Sacrament to be effective for the person who receives it?

2. In your opinion, what is the value of outward preparations for Communion, such as going well-dressed to the worship service?

Are You Ready?

St. Paul's words in 1 Corinthians are clear and forceful. But sometimes, they almost frighten people into avoiding Communion for fear of doing something wrong. That, obviously, is not Scripture's intent. As we have seen, God encourages us to commune frequently. The Lord's Supper is a celebration for every believing heart.

Three questions can help us examine our beliefs. They can easily be asked and answered as part of our preparation for coming to the Lord's Table. Just take a look at your past, present, and future.

1. Am I sorry for my sins?
2. Do I believe that Jesus Christ is my Savior?
3. Will I, through the Holy Spirit's help, try to avoid the sins I am guilty of and live more according to His will?

A simple affirmative answer to these questions will prepare your heart.

To Review and Remember

Examine yourselves, to see whether you are in the faith. Test yourselves. *2 Corinthians 13:5*

How to Receive This Sacrament Worthily

55 Confirmation—A Life Blessed by God

I Am a Child of God

What is the story of your spiritual journey? Were you baptized as a baby? Did you receive the blessings of Baptism later in your childhood? Those baptized as infants receive the gift of faith, and others speak for them. You are now old enough to speak for yourself and confess Christ in your own words. Before long, you will stand before God's altar on your Confirmation Day and restate or affirm the faith the Holy Spirit worked in you at your Baptism. This you will do by your own choice, just as you will freely decide when to come to the Lord's Supper. As you prepare for confirmation, you will want to think through what you will say and promise as you are confirmed.

Catechism Question 306 defines confirmation as "a public rite of the church preceded by a period of instruction designed to help baptized Christians identify with the life and mission of the Christian community. Note: Prior to admission to the Lord's Supper, it is necessary to be instructed in the Christian faith (1 Corinthians 11:28). The rite of confirmation provides an opportunity for the individual Christian, relying on God's promise given in Holy Baptism, to make a personal public confession of the faith and a lifelong pledge of fidelity to Christ."

1. Write one or two of God's promises that are most important to you.

2. Write a sentence summarizing your plan of life-long faithfulness to Christ.

Alive in the Means of Grace

Scripture tells us that the Holy Spirit works through *the Word of God, Holy Baptism, and the Lord's Supper,* through which He brings us to, and keeps us in, the saving faith. We call these visible actions of God the *Means of Grace.*

1. The Holy Spirit strengthens your faith whenever you prayerfully read, listen, think, or talk about the teachings of Scripture.
a. Read Hebrews 4:12. To what is God's Word compared?

b. How does the power of the Spirit, through the Word, work in your life?

2. Your Baptism may have happened a long time ago. We have already learned that in Baptism we receive the Holy Spirit to rescue us from three enemies—sin, death, and the power of the devil. But Baptism is involved in our lives now. Martin Luther once said that when He felt the assault of the devil upon his soul, he would remind himself that he was God's child through Baptism. What do each of the following verses remind us about our new life in Christ, the life into which we have been baptized?

a. Romans 6:3–4

b. Romans 8:38–39

3. Read 1 Corinthians 10:16–17. Identify the specific things that happen when attending the Lord's Supper.

4. Now, as a newly confirmed believer in Christ, what are some things you can do to
a. continue growing in your faith?

b. serve in your congregation and stay connected to the Body of Christ?

c. participate in mission projects abroad?

5. Place a star behind those items in the preceding exercise that have been a part of your life during the past week.

To Review and Remember

Be faithful unto death, and I will give you the crown of life. *Revelation 2:10*

So everyone who acknowledges Me before men, I also will acknowledge before My Father who is in heaven, but whoever denies Me before men, I also will deny before My Father who is in heaven. *Matthew 10:32–33*

56 Daily Devotions, Part 1: Morning and Evening Prayers

Evening Prayers and Morning Joy

Our loving heavenly Father invites us to communicate with Him constantly. We read in 1 Thessalonians 5:17–18: "Pray without ceasing, give thanks in all circumstances; for this is the will of God in Christ Jesus for you." Acts 16:23–34 tells of a time when Paul and Silas were imprisoned in Philippi for preaching the Gospel. Review this account and answer the following questions.

1. After talking to God the Father at the beginning and closing of the day, Luther suggests that the child of God can know joy and good cheer. What evidence do we have that Paul and Silas knew joy because of God's love for them in Christ Jesus, even after being arrested, flogged, and shackled (v. 25)?

2. What two opportunities did God give Paul and Silas to share their faith with unbelievers?

3. Identify the person experiencing joy and the source of joy during the early morning hours at the conclusion of the account (v. 34).

4. Under what circumstances might praying provide you with an opportunity to share your faith with others?

Daily Prayers

Martin Luther recognized the importance of prayer in the life of a Christian. When he wrote the Small Catechism in 1529, Luther included a Morning and Evening Prayer for God's people to use at the beginning and ending of each day. Review these prayers and respond to the following questions.

1. Why is it important for the head of the family to teach the household to pray?

2. Tell briefly how each of the following relate to the everyday life of the believer.

a. Making the sign of the cross

b. Saying, "In the name of the Father and of the Son and of the Holy Spirit. Amen."

c. Repeating the Apostles' Creed

d. Repeating the Lord's Prayer

3. Luther designed his Morning and Evening Prayers to open and close each day in close communication with our Father in heaven.

a. How are the Morning and Evening Prayers alike?

b. How do the Morning and Evening Prayers differ?

How the head of the family should teach his household to pray morning and evening

Morning Prayer

In the morning when you get up, make the sign of the holy cross and say:

In the name of the Father and of the ✝ Son and of the Holy Spirit. Amen.

Then, kneeling or standing, repeat the Creed and the Lord's Prayer. If you choose, you may also say this little prayer:

I thank You, my heavenly Father, through Jesus Christ, Your dear Son, that You have kept me this night from all harm and danger; and I pray that You would keep me this day also from sin and every evil, that all my doings and life may please You. For into Your hands I commend myself, my body and soul, and all things. Let Your holy angel be with me, that the evil foe may have no power over me. Amen.

Then go joyfully to your work, singing a hymn, like that of the Ten Commandments, or whatever your devotion may suggest.

Evening Prayer

In the evening when you go to bed, make the sign of the holy cross and say:

In the name of the Father and of the ✝ Son and of the Holy Spirit. Amen.

Then kneeling or standing, repeat the Creed and the Lord's Prayer. If you choose you may also say this little prayer:

I thank You, my heavenly Father, through Jesus Christ, Your dear Son, that You have graciously kept me this day; and I pray that You would forgive me all my sins where I have done wrong, and graciously keep me this night. For into Your hands I commend myself, my body and soul, and all things. Let Your holy angel be with me, that the evil foe may have no power over me. Amen.

Then go to sleep at once and in good cheer.

To Review and Remember

By day the LORD commands His steadfast love, and at night His song is with me, a prayer to the God of my life. *Psalm 42:8*

The steadfast love of the LORD never ceases; his mercies never come to an end; they are new every morning. *Lamentations 3:22–23a*

Luther's Morning Prayer

Luther's Evening Prayer

57 Daily Devotions, Part 2: Table Prayers

How the head of the family should teach his household to ask a blessing and return thanks

Asking a Blessing

The children and members of the household shall go to the table reverently, fold their hands, and say:

The eyes of all look to You, [O Lord,] and You give them their food at the proper time. You open Your hand and satisfy the desires of every living thing. [Psalm 145:15–16]

Then shall be said the Lord's Prayer and the following:

Lord God, heavenly Father, bless us and these Your gifts which we receive from Your bountiful goodness, through Jesus Christ, our Lord. Amen.

Returning Thanks

Also, after eating, they shall, in like manner, reverently and with folded hands say:

Give thanks to the Lord, for He is good. His love endures forever. [He] gives food to every creature. He provides food for the cattle and for the young ravens when they call. His pleasure is not in the strength of the horse, nor His delight in the legs of a man; the Lord delights in those who fear Him, who put their hope in His unfailing love. [Psalm 136:1, 25; 147:9–11]

Then shall be said the Lord's Prayer and the following:

We thank You, Lord God, heavenly Father, for all Your benefits, through Jesus Christ, our Lord, who lives and reigns with You and the Holy Spirit forever and ever. Amen.

Imagine This

Three times a day, seven children sit at the kitchen table with their father and enjoy delicious meals. They live in a beautiful home their father cares for, they spend the money he gives to them, and they wear the clothes he provides for them. But at the table and throughout the day, the children ignore their father. They never tell him how much they enjoy all the

beautiful things he gives to them. They never share with him the disappointments, joys, and hopes of their days. They talk with him only when they are in trouble or when they can't find the solution to a problem on their own.

How is our relationship with God sometimes like the relationship the children in the story have with their father? How does the Holy Spirit move us to act differently than the children in the story?

Our Generous Heavenly Father

In his epistle, James talks about God, the giver of all good things. He writes, "Every good gift and every perfect gift is from above, coming down from the Father of lights with whom there is no variance or shadow due to change. Of His own will He brought us forth by the word of truth, that we should be a kind of firstfruits of His creatures" (1:17–18).

1. What quality of God does James specifically mention?

2. What kind of birth does James speak of in these verses? See 1 Peter 1:23–25.

3. Name five good things for which you are especially thankful today.

In a Spirit of Thankfulness

In the Daily Prayers section of the Small Catechism, Martin Luther encourages the head of the household to teach everyone in the household to ask God's blessing on the food and to give thanks on receiving it. See the section from the Catechism that is reproduced in this lesson.

1. Are the folding of hands and bowing of head in prayer important prayer postures for adults as well as children? What other ways could we focus our attention or show reverence during prayer?

a. Matthew 14:13–21

b. Matthew 26:26–28

Mealtime Prayers

We who are called such [Christians] and desire to be considered such should take this to heart: We should receive our gifts from God almighty with reverence and thanksgiving and not go to the table as pigs to the trough and leave the table, after we have taken our fill, without thanking our good God with the slightest little prayer or whisper, nay, without ever thinking of our Lord God, who feeds us ingrates out of pure mercy and kind benevolence. So we forget our good God, who richly offers us all sorts of things for our enjoyment. (Martin Luther, *What Luther Says*, compiled by Ewald M. Plass [St. Louis: Concordia Publishing House, 1959], § 3459)

2. Is it necessary to kneel when we pray?

3. Luther also suggests praying the Lord's Prayer at mealtime. Why is the Lord's Prayer so special to the people of God? See Luke 11:1–4.

1. Dr. Luther once reflected on the spirit of thankfulness evidenced in regular mealtime prayers in the comments on Deuteronomy 8:10 that he wrote in the margins of someone's Bible. Read Luther's note above. Look up Deuteronomy 8:10, and write it below Luther's comment.
2. On a separate sheet, write the prayers you commonly speak before and after meals or write mealtime prayers of your own.

4. Review the Fourth Petition of to the Lord's Prayer and its explanation. For what two reasons do we pray "Give us this day our daily bread"?

To Review and Remember

Oh give thanks to the LORD; call upon His name; make known His deeds among the peoples! *1 Chronicles 16:8*

You cause the grass to grow for the livestock and plants for man to cultivate, that he may bring forth food from the earth. *Psalm 104:14*

Asking a Blessing

Returning Thanks

5. On several occasions, Jesus modeled for us the practice of thanking God for our food. Perhaps Jesus used some of the same words from Holy Scripture that we use in our table prayers. Consider the following examples. What miraculous event takes place at each event?

58 Table of Duties, Part 1: Relating to Others in Church and State

God's Word on Christian Vocation

God's Kingdom of Grace—The Church

Place a letter in each blank below to match the statement with the passage from God's Word at right to which it most directly refers.

> **Table of Duties**
> Certain Passages of Scripture for Various Holy Orders and Positions, Admonishing Them about Their Duties and Responsibilities

___1. God's Word warns that those new to the faith should not immediately become pastors.

___2. Through sound teaching, pastors are equipped to encourage others with a true interpretation of God's Word and to counter those whose teachings are false.

___3. God calls on pastors to model Christian love and faithfulness in the relationships they build with their wives and children.

___4. God's people are to respect their pastors, to love them, and to live peaceably with one another.

___5. Those properly instructed in the teachings of God's Word are called on to share good things with their instructor.

___6. God would have us compensate those who preach the Good News.

___7. Those who preach and teach deserve double honor and reasonable wages.

___8. God would have us obey our pastors so that their work among us will be a joy and not a burden.

To Bishops, Pastors, and Preachers

a. The overseer must be above reproach, the husband of but one wife, temperate, self-controlled, respectable, hospitable, able to teach, not given to drunkenness, not violent but gentle, not quarrelsome, not a lover of money. He must manage his own family well and see that his children obey him with proper respect. **1 Timothy 3:2–4**

b. He must not be a recent convert, or he may become conceited and fall under the same judgment as the devil. **1 Timothy 3:6**

c. He must hold firmly to the trustworthy message as it has been taught, so that he can encourage others by sound doctrine and refute those who oppose it. **Titus 1:9**

What the Hearers Owe Their Pastors

d. The Lord has commanded that those who preach the gospel should receive their living from the gospel. **1 Corinthians 9:14**

e. Anyone who receives instruction in the word must share all good things with his instructor. Do not be deceived: God cannot be mocked. A man reaps what he sows. **Galatians 6:6–7**

f. The elders who direct the affairs of the church well are worthy of double honor, especially those whose work is preaching and teaching. For the Scripture says, "Do not muzzle the ox while it is treading out the grain," and "The worker deserves his wages." **1 Timothy 5:17–18**

g. We ask you, brothers, to respect those who work hard among you, who are over you in the Lord and who admonish you. Hold them in the highest regard in love because of their work. Live in peace with each other. **1 Thessalonians 5:12–13**

h. Obey your leaders and submit to their authority. They keep watch over you as men who must give an account. Obey them so that their work will be a joy, not a burden, for that would be of no advantage to you. **Hebrews 13:17**

God's Kingdom of Power— The Government

As citizens of an earthly government, we have the responsibility to be informed and current on local, national, and worldwide issues, and we must vote. We should do our utmost to obey the laws instituted by the government, including traffic and tax laws.

Match the statements with the passage to which it most directly refers.

Of Civil Government

a. Everyone must submit himself to the governing authorities, for there is no authority except that which God has established. . . . Consequently, he who rebels against the authority is rebelling against what God has instituted, and those who do so will bring judgment on themselves. . . . For he is God's servant to do you good. **Romans 13:1–4**

Of Citizens

b. Give to Caesar what is Caesar's, and to God what is God's. **Matthew 22:21**

c. This is also why you pay taxes, for the authorities are God's servants, who give their full time to governing. Give everyone what you owe him: If you owe taxes, pay taxes; if revenue, then revenue; if respect, then respect; if honor, then honor. **Romans 13:5–7**

d. I urge, then, first of all, that requests, prayers, intercession and thanksgiving be made for everyone—for kings and all those in authority, that we may live peaceful and quiet lives in all godliness and holiness. This is good, and pleases God our Savior. **1 Timothy 2:1–3**

e. Remind the people to be subject to rulers and authorities, to be obedient, to be ready to do whatever is good. **Titus 3:1**

f. Submit yourselves for the Lord's sake to every authority instituted among men: . . . who are sent by him to punish those who do wrong and to commend those who do right. **1 Peter 2:13–14**

___1. God would have us pray with thanksgiving on behalf of our rulers and others in authority over us and to lead peaceful and quiet lives.

___2. For our Lord's sake, God desires us to obey those in authority over us. God has established authorities to punish wrongdoers and uphold those who do right.

___3. Because God has established authority, rebelling against authority is rebelling against what God has instituted. Those God has placed in positions of authority are God's servants.

___4. God would have us be subject to and obey our authorities and to be ready to do good.

___5. God's people are to pay taxes and to give to everyone what is owed.

___6. Christians are to give to the government what is required and to give to God what God requires.

Thanks Be to God for His Good Gifts

We don't always appreciate the blessings God has given us through our pastors and rulers or through our church and the secular government. We may complain or show disrespect. Jesus earned forgiveness for these and all other sins on Calvary's cross. Working through God's Word, His Holy Spirit helps us to honor those whom God has given to serve in authority over us. Consider the following items. Write *church* before each item referring to a blessing God gives us through the church. Write *state* before each item identifying a blessing God provides us through our secular government.

_____ 1. Criminals are punished.

_____ 2. Citizens' rights are protected.

_____ 3. People receive the assurance that God in Christ has forgiven their sins through confession and absolution.

_____ 4. Wars are waged for our protection.

_____ 5. God's Word is preached in its truth and purity.

_____ 6. The Sacraments are administered.

_____ 7. Christian education and mission efforts bring people the Gospel.

To Review and Remember

Remind them to be submissive to rulers and authorities, to be obedient, to be ready for every good work. *Titus 3:1*

We must obey God rather than men. *Acts 5:29*

He [Christ] gave the apostles, the prophets, the evangelists, the shepherds and teachers, to equip the saints for the work of ministry. *Ephesians 4:11–12*

The Fourth Commandment and its explanation

59 Table of Duties, Part 2: Relating within the Family

Two Truths and a Lie

Read Colossians 3:17–25, and then respond to the following three statements. Which ones are true? Which one is a lie?

___1. The Lord tells us we should work heartily in whatever we do, as though we were working for the Lord.

___2. Wives, husbands, children, and slaves must all work in their God-given positions or roles to serve one another.

___3. When we serve other people, we are not serving Christ.

Serving God in My Vocation

Each of us have vocations, or God-given callings in our lives. Some vocations we are "born into." We are a son or daughter because we are born into a family. Other vocations come by choice. Eventually, you will complete your education and move into a career in which you'll serve your neighbors and, thereby, will serve God as well. We're all hearers and students of God's Word and receivers of God's gracious gifts.

Martin Luther, in the Table of Duties, uses Scripture to point out ways God's people can respond in actions of love toward their family members. God's Word teaches that followers of Jesus put their faith into action as the Holy Spirit strengthens, encourages, and empowers them in Word and Sacrament.

To Husbands

Husbands, in the same way be considerate as you live with your wives, and treat them with respect as the weaker partner and as heirs with you of the gracious gift of life, so that nothing will hinder your prayers. **1 Peter 3:7**

Husbands, love your wives and do not be harsh with them. **Colossians 3:19**

To Wives

Wives, submit to your husbands as to the Lord. **Ephesians 5:22**

They were submissive to their own husbands, like Sarah, who obeyed Abraham and called him her master. You are her daughters if you do what is right and do not give way to fear. **1 Peter 3:5–6**

To Parents

Fathers, do not exasperate your children; instead, bring them up in the training and instruction of the Lord. **Ephesians 6:4**

To Children

Children, obey your parents in the Lord, for this is right. "Honor your father and mother"—which is the first commandment with a promise—"that it may go well with you and that you may enjoy long life on the earth." **Ephesians 6:1–3**

Complete the following matching exercise to indicate how God's Spirit enabled these people to show God's love to their families.

a. Abram (Genesis 13:8–18)

b. Miriam (Exodus 2:1–10)

c. Jethro (Exodus 18:7–24)

d. David (1 Samuel 17:17–20)

e. Andrew (John 1:35–42)

_____1. In joyful obedience to his father, this child brought food to his siblings.

_____2. This uncle allowed his nephew his choice of the land in order to keep peace in the family.

_____3. This sibling kept watch over a baby brother as he floated in a basket.

_____4. This young man brought his brother to someone who changed his life.

_____5. This father-in-law gave sound advice on how to lead the people of God.

Showing God's Love to My Family in a Sinful World

Because we live in a sin-filled world, it is not always easy to react to family members with Christlike love. Your family might irritate you, let you down, or hurt your feelings. You might sin against your family too. But remember, we serve more than just our families in our vocations at home. We also serve God. As Christians, we realize that we are indeed sinful, and God's Word proclaims the beautiful Gospel message of forgiveness of sins and salvation through Jesus Christ alone. In response to this awesome, liberating message, we can do our jobs at home not just because we feel like we have to, but because we want to. In even the littlest household chores, we can serve God. Colossians 3:23 encourages us, saying, "Whatever you do, work heartily, as for the Lord and not for men." The Holy Spirit gives us the strength to respond to God's great love for us by sharing His love with our families by the way we act. Write some ways that you, through the power of the Holy Spirit, can respond in love toward family members in the following situations:

1. Your dad told you to clean your room before company comes over. You don't want to do it—after all, they won't be spending time in your room.

2. Mom came home from work looking really tired.

3. Your sister came home from school with puffy red eyes and tear-stained cheeks.

4. Someone accidentally deleted some of your homework assignments from the computer, and you need them!

To Review and Remember

We love because He first loved us. If anyone says, "I love God," and hates his brother, he is a liar; for he who does not love his brother whom he has seen cannot love God whom he has not seen. And this commandment we have from Him: whoever loves God must also love his brother. *1 John 4:19–21*

Whatever you do, work heartily, as for the Lord and not for men. *Colossians 3:23*

60 Table of Duties, Part 3: Relating to Everyone

Faith and Love: The Summary of Christian Doctrine

Martin Luther once said that all of Scripture teaches two things—receiving benefactions from God (faith) and conferring them on our neighbor (love). He added that it is impossible for one to exist without the other, and that the firmer one believes, the more diligent and willing one is to help one's neighbor. Fill in the blanks below with either *Faith* or *Love* to identify the principle about which the statement more closely refers.

1. _____ gives us all we truly need.

2. _____ gives us the desire to share all things with others.

3. _____ makes us children of God and heirs of heaven.

4. _____ moves us to help and defend the lowliest and neediest.

5. Through _____, we receive gifts from God above.

6. Through _____ , we give God's gifts to those around us.

7. Because we received _____ , we respond in actions of _____ toward others.

Putting Faith and Love into Action

In the Table of Duties, Martin Luther has identified a number of ways the people of God can respond in actions of love to those around them. God's Word teaches that followers of Jesus put their faith into action as the Holy Spirit works in them through the Word and Sacraments.

Write the letter that identifies each portion of the Table of Duties (found on the next page) before the statement to which it most closely applies.

___1. God's Spirit empowers and motivates those in authority to motivate kindly those who are their subordinates, remembering that all of us have one mighty Superior in heaven who shows no partiality toward us.

___ 2. By God's power, those who are alone are to hope in God and be constantly in prayer, asking God for help.

___ 3. God would have us treat all others with the care and concern we have for our own bodies.

___ 4. God desires employees and persons under the authority of others to honor, respect, and be obedient toward their superiors, serving and working for them to the best of their ability as if they were working for our Lord and Savior, Jesus Christ.

___ 5. By God's grace, young people submit to their elders and relate to one another in humility.

___ 6. God's people come before His throne of grace with prayers for all others.

___ 7. Those families that learn God's Word together and put it into practice receive the blessings God promises.

To Workers of All Kinds

a. Slaves, obey your earthly masters with respect and fear, and with sincerity of heart, just as you would obey Christ. Obey them not only to win their favor when their eye is on you, but like slaves of Christ, doing the will of God from your heart. Serve wholeheartedly, as if you were serving the Lord, not men, because you know that the Lord will reward everyone for whatever good he does, whether he is slave or free. **Ephesians 6:5–8**

To Employers and Supervisors

b. Masters, treat your slaves in the same way. Do not threaten them, since you know that he who is both their Master and yours is in heaven, and there is no favoritism with Him. **Ephesians 6:9**

To Youth

c. Young men, in the same way be submissive to those who are older. All of you, clothe yourselves with humility toward one another, because, "God opposes the proud but gives grace to the humble." Humble yourselves, therefore, under God's mighty hand, that He may lift you up in due time. **1 Peter 5:5–6**

To Widows

d. The widow who is really in need and left all alone puts her hope in God and continues night and day to pray and to ask God for help. But the widow who lives for pleasure is dead even while she lives. **1 Timothy 5:5–6**

To Everyone

e. The commandments . . . are summed up in this one rule: "Love your neighbor as yourself." **Romans 13:9**

f. I urge . . . that requests, prayers, intercession and thanksgiving be made for everyone. **1 Timothy 2:1**

g. *Let each his lesson learn with care, and all the household well shall fare.*

Reflections on Living and Giving

Jesus described the judgment of the faithful as follows:

[31]When the Son of Man comes in His glory, and all the angels with Him, then He will sit on His glorious throne. [32]Before Him will be gathered all the nations, and He will separate people one from another as a shepherd separates the sheep from the goats. [33]And He will place the sheep on His right, but the goats on the left.

[34]Then the King will say to those on His right, "Come, you who are blessed by My Father, inherit the kingdom prepared for you from the foundation of the world. [35]For I was hungry and you gave Me food, I was thirsty and you gave Me drink, I was a stranger and you welcomed Me, [36]I was naked and you clothed Me, I was sick and you visited Me, I was in prison and you came to Me."

[37]Then the righteous will answer Him, saying, "Lord, when did we see You hungry and feed You, or thirsty and give You drink? [38]And when did we see You a stranger and welcome You, or naked and clothe You? [39]And when did we see You sick or in prison and visit You?"

[40]And the King will answer them, "Truly, I say to you, as you did it to one of the least of these My brothers, you did it to Me." (Matthew 25:31–40)

1. What qualifies people to receive their inheritance as sons of God and brothers of Jesus Christ? See Ephesians 1:3–8, especially verse 7.

2. What do the questions asked of the King tell you about the people's acts of love and kindness toward others?

3. Explain the meaning of "Christlike" implied in Matthew 25:40.

To Review and Remember

[Jesus said,] "A new commandment I give to you, that you love one another: just as I have loved you, you also are to love one another. By this all people will know that you are My disciples, if you have love for one another." *John 13:34–35*

In this is love, not that we have loved God but that He loved us and sent His Son to be the propitiation for our sins. Beloved, if God so loved us, we also ought to love one another. *1 John 4:10–11*